"IN A SINGLE GARMENT OF DESTINY"

"IN A SINGLE GARMENT OF DESTINY"

A Global Vision of Justice

MARTIN LUTHER KING, JR.

Edited and Introduced by Lewis V. Baldwin

Foreword by Charlayne Hunter-Gault

BEACON PRESS

BOSTON

BEACON PRESS
25 Beacon Street
Boston, Massachusetts 02108–2892

Beacon Press books are published under the auspices of the
Unitarian Universalist Association of Congregations.

Beacon Press gratefully acknowledges the
Unitarian Universalist Veatch Program at Shelter Rock for
its generous support of the King Legacy series.

 In Association With

"The King Legacy" is a federally registered trademark of
the Unitarian Universalist Association Corporation.

Obvious typographical errors in transcriptions of spoken-word
materials were corrected to aid in ease of reading. All other errors or
stylistic inconsistencies have been retained in their original form.

Printed in the United States of America

15 14 13 12   8 7 6 5 4 3 2 1

Text design by Wilsted & Taylor Publishing Services

Library of Congress Cataloging-in-Publication data
can be found on page 228.

As we grow and come to see the oneness of mankind and the geographical oneness of the world, made possible by man's scientific and technological ingenuity, more and more we are going to have to try to see our oneness in terms of brotherhood. This does not mean that everyone has to agree at every point. There can be a world government where diversity can exist and this would lessen many tensions that we face today, and it would also enable everybody to understand that we are clothed in a single garment of destiny, and whatever affects one nation directly in the world, indirectly affects all.

—Martin Luther King, Jr., *Redbook Magazine*,
November 5, 1964

CONTENTS

PART II

Confronting the Color Bar:
Overcoming Racism as a World Problem

PART III
Breaking the Chains of Colonialism:
The Rise of Peoples of Color in the Third World

PART VI

Toward a Positive Pluralism:
Interfaith Dialogue and Global Community

FOREWORD

CHARLAYNE HUNTER-GAULT

When I first met Dr. Martin Luther King in Atlanta in the early 1960s, during the heady days of the civil rights movement, recognition of each other was instantaneous. Though there was no blood connection, we were family. Not only were we joined in the "beloved community" he often talked about—people fighting for freedom, justice, and equality in the Jim Crow South—but we were also family in the sense that we shared the bond of values taught in our homes and communities, values that were timeless and transcendent, values that overcame the efforts of the white South to deny us our rights and that gave us a first-class sense of ourselves. So, when Dr. King spoke, it was as if I were hearing an older brother nurtured in the same values pulpit as I was.

Like Dr. King, I learned many verses from the Bible and was taught from it. One of the most enduring lessons came from Proverbs 22:6: "Train up a child in the way he should go, and when he is old he will not depart from it." When those like me, who came of age in the civil rights movement, fought the lie of "separate but equal," the vision and hope of Dr. King helped to keep us fighting. Dr. King exemplified this not only through his eloquent witness but also through his personal sacrifice, including joining in the student protests in my hometown of Atlanta that led to his arrest and to a sentence, based on a trumped-up charge, that was longer than that of any of the others arrested.

Clearly, my generation marched to its own drummer but we also followed the tune of Dr. King, a "drum major for justice" who, some six years before the birth of the civil rights movement and just as the U.S. Supreme Court was outlawing "separate but equal" in its 1954 *Brown v. Board* decision, spoke these visionary words at a National Baptist Convention:

> Frequently there appears on the stage of history individuals who have the insight to look beyond the inadequacies

of the old order and see the necessity for the new. These are the persons with a sort of divine discontent. They realize that the world as it is is far from the world that it ought to be. They never confuse the "isness" of an old order with the "oughtness" of a new order. And so in every age and every generation there are those persons who have envisioned some new order.

Thus, with his words, as well as his deeds, Dr. King helped "train us up in the way we should go," empowering a generation to see the things it had not yet learned to see and to open its eyes to an even bigger prize than the elimination of Jim Crow. That's why when we faced the terrifying presence of the Ku Klux Klan and their ilk, we would chant: "King is our leader, [Donald] Hollowell is our lawyer, and we shall not be moved."

More than a decade after delivering that speech, Dr. King had matured along with his vision, which he articulated in a prophetic piece titled "The World House."

However deeply American Negroes are caught in the struggle to be at last at home in our homeland of the United States, we cannot ignore the larger world house in which we are also dwellers. Equality with whites will not solve the problems of either whites or Negroes if it means equality in a world society stricken by poverty and in a universe doomed to extinction by war. All inhabitants of the globe are now neighbors.

He foresaw the need to focus on the issues affecting the beloved community both within and beyond our borders, issues we still confront: the legacy of slavery and segregation, of colonialism and apartheid, of injustice and inequality, of racism, and of the devastation of war and economic inequality.

Some of the children of the civil rights movement, such as Bob Moses, who toiled in the backwaters of the South registering voters until freedom rang there, heard the call and moved to Africa, which was struggling to overcome colonialism or the legacy of injustice fostered by that system. Others joined in the protests to end apartheid in South Africa. Thanks to this remarkable collection, we learn that Dr. King addressed this evil empire as early as 1957, when he joined with Eleanor Roosevelt and Bishop James Pike in a Declaration of Conscience to protest the inhumanity of apartheid. Such public denunciations clearly inspired others to follow, including young artists such as Gil Scott-Heron, who wrote the 1976 song "Johannesburg" ("Tell me Brother, have you heard? Johannesburg . . . Glad to see resistance growin'"), and Randall Robinson and thousands of others, like a young Barack Obama, who joined in anti-apartheid protests of the 1980s, which ultimately saw Nelson Mandela and his people freed.

During that time, as I had reached one mountaintop, fulfilling my dream of becoming a journalist, my journey to the next mountaintop took me first to South Africa to help expose further the lingering effects of the wrongs of apartheid and later to other places throughout our global neighborhood where people of all colors, races, and creeds were yearning to breathe free. And though Dr. King was vilified for his vision at the time, children of the civil rights movement, such as Julian Bond, continued their journey to the next mountaintop by joining Dr. King in protesting America's misguided involvement in the Vietnam War and embracing "the human family," including those whose appearance but little else was different from their own.

And today, *a luta continua*—"the struggle continues"—in the countries on the African continent, some are taking baby steps toward democracy; others are not yet there in the countries of the Arab Spring, in the war-torn nations of Iraq, Afghanistan, and Pakistan. Women may hold up half the sky, as the saying goes, but they are still not recognized for it in all too many societies. And in even the most mature democracies, the economic justice championed by Dr. King is still proving elusive, creating "ticking time bombs," especially among unemployed youth all over the worldwide neighborhood. None of these problems can be solved without a global vision and global action. And though the words "we shall overcome someday" were sung with earnest conviction by Dr. King and his followers, Dr. King also spoke of "the fierce urgency of now."

Dr. King's teachings from pulpits and podiums helped prepare me and many of my peers for our ongoing journey to the "worldwide neighborhood." And though only select audiences heard him as far back as 1954, thanks to *"In a Single Garment of Destiny": A Global Vision of Justice*, we now have a unique collection that supplies the proof of Dr. King's prescience. Dr. King's words, captured in this enduring collection, continue to train us up in the way we should go.

EDITOR'S NOTE

I was extremely selective and thoughtful in the selection of documents in *"In a Single Garment of Destiny."* Because King often used much of the same content in his sermons, speeches, and writings on global concerns such as racial oppression, poverty and economic exploitation, war and human destruction, and religious bigotry and intolerance, the process proved all the more difficult. Ultimately, the decision was to select material that reflected the interplay or interconnectedness of these concerns in King's consciousness, and also his perspective on and contributions to world liberation movements.

The content of this volume rests on the conviction that understanding the global King solely on the basis of one set of sources, such as his sermons or speeches, is woefully inadequate. King's image as an international figure and thinker is best understood through the full range of his oral and written sources. The documents here cover the spectrum, from articles, statements, letters, and brief comments to sermons, speeches, and addresses. Joint statements that emerged out of King's collaboration with other national leaders, such as Eleanor Roosevelt and Bishop James A. Pike, and world leaders, like Albert J. Luthuli and Thich Nhat Hanh, are also included, for they reinforce the sense of King as one who personified, in word and deed, the concept of an interrelated and interdependent world. In other words, the joint statements prove that King went beyond merely articulating a world vision and producing oral and written statements on world problems to actually collaborating with national and world leaders in translating that vision into practical reality. Without these joint statements, something of the global King gets lost.

The documents provided here came essentially from four locations: the Library and Archives of the Martin Luther King, Jr., Center for Nonviolent Social Change in Atlanta, Georgia; the Martin Luther King, Jr., Collection at Morehouse College in

Atlanta; Special Collections at the Mugar Memorial Library at Boston University in Massachusetts; and the collection housed by the Martin Luther King, Jr., Papers Project at Stanford University in California. Most of King's personal papers can be found at these locations. Staff persons at all of these locations were helpful in identifying, verifying, and providing a range of King materials.

The documents are included in *"In a Single Garment of Destiny"* without major changes. Readers will discover that King was often repetitive when writing or speaking on global matters, but this, too, yields insight into the spirit of the man and the consistency with which he adhered to and expressed certain ideas, concepts, and principles. (Even so, I have endeavored not to include materials that use a lot of the very same content.)

When read properly, these documents lead to a new understanding and appreciation of King's thought and contributions to the emergence and shaping of the modern, globalized world. As an intellectual and activist, the phenomenal figure of Martin Luther King, Jr., looms large over the whole contemporary horizon, and his values, gifts, insights, and convictions still inform global thinking and crusades for human liberation and empowerment.

GENERAL INTRODUCTION

This is a new kind of book about the world vision of Martin Luther King, Jr. Too many people continue to think of Dr. King as "a southern civil rights leader" or "an American Gandhi," thus ignoring his impact on poor and oppressed people everywhere. *"In a Single Garment of Destiny"* is the first book to treat King's positions on global liberation struggles through the prism of his own words and activities. The purpose is not only celebration but also a critical engagement with a towering figure whose ideas and social praxis have become so significant in the reshaping of the modern world.

King's interest in the problems of the poor and oppressed worldwide was evident long before he achieved national and international prominence. He came out of a family background that encouraged a concern for world affairs. His own father, Martin Luther King, Sr., the distinguished pastor of the Ebenezer Baptist Church in Atlanta, Georgia, communicated with black South African activists and addressed the problems of racism and poverty in America and in other lands when King, Jr., was a child. Inspired by this family tradition, King, Jr., at age fifteen, in a high school speech called "The Negro and the Constitution," spoke of the resonating irony of an America claiming freedom while denying basic rights to blacks, and also referred to the United States' moral responsibility in a world that threatened the true flowering of democracy. As a student at Atlanta's Morehouse College and at Crozer Theological Seminary in Pennsylvania in the late 1940s and early 1950s, King, Jr., came to the conclusion that blacks in America would not win genuine freedom as long as peoples of color abroad suffered on grounds of race and economics.

King had experiences in Montgomery, Alabama, that not only increased his interest in international events but also solidified his commitment to ending racism, poverty, colonialism, war, and other social evils that disproportionately afflicted black Americans and peoples in the so-called Third World. While serving as pastor of Montgomery's Dexter Avenue Baptist Church from 1954 to 1959, King occasionally drew parallels between white racism in the United States and European colonialism in Africa, Asia, and Latin America, and it was his conviction that the black struggle in the Jim Crow South had much to contribute to and learn from movements for independence abroad. This conviction matured during the Montgomery bus boycott in 1955 and 1956, and was significantly reinforced when King attended the independence celebrations in Ghana at the request of Prime Minister Kwame Nkrumah in March 1957 and visited India, "the land of Gandhi," in 1959. Animated by his experiences and travels abroad, in the late 1950s King actually joined the American Committee on Africa (ACOA), a New York–based organization of Christian pacifists who contributed to freedom movements inside South Africa and who advocated nonviolent approaches in the assault on systems of oppression everywhere.

The 1960s brought similar involvements on King's part. Although his work through his Southern Christian Leadership Conference (SCLC), the ACOA, and the American Negro Leadership Conference on Africa (ANLCA) are more widely known, he also endorsed and supported numerous organizations throughout the world that contributed financially, morally, and in other ways to freedom movements. King actually combined such activities with a powerful and consistent advocacy for world peace in pulpits throughout America and in other parts of the world. As far back as the late 1950s, he had called for the total eradication of war and, by the early 1960s, had signed numerous statements with other liberal Americans condemning nuclear testing. By the time of his death, in April 1968, King had become completely convinced that the achievement of world peace and community hinged on the elimination of what he called "the world's three greatest social evils"; namely, racism, poverty, and war. (See part I, "All of God's Children: Toward a Global Vision of Human Liberation.")

More specifics on how King sought to connect the civil rights movement with freedom struggles abroad would be helpful here in grasping the depth of his belief in global liberation, or what he called "the world house" or "a new world order." In July 1957, King joined Eleanor Roosevelt and Bishop James A. Pike as initial sponsors, under the auspices of the ACOA, of the worldwide Declaration of Conscience, a document included in this volume. The declaration proclaimed December 10, 1957, Human Rights Day, as a day to protest against the organized inhumanity of the South African government and its racial-apartheid policies, and it urged churches, universities, trade unions, business and professional organizations, veterans groups, and members of all other free associations to devote the day to prayer, demonstrations, acts of civil disobedience, and other forms of nonviolent protest. The Declaration of Conscience, signed by heads of state, religious leaders, and scholars, actually symbolized, perhaps more than anything else, King's efforts to establish links between the struggle in the American South and the black South African anti-apartheid cause.

In July 1962, King and the black South African leader Albert J. Luthuli became cosponsors, under the banner of the ACOA, of the worldwide Appeal for Action Against Apartheid, a declaration also included in this book. This crusade was in the nature of a follow-up to the global effort of 1957. King and Luthuli, both ministers and activists committed to nonviolence, had communicated with each other through the mail since the late 1950s, and, although they never met, they shared a commitment to the poor and the oppressed everywhere, or what King called "the least of these." The Appeal for Action Against Apartheid called upon churches, unions, lodges, clubs, and other groups and associations to make December 10, 1962, Human Rights Day, a day for meetings, protest, and prayer, and to urge their governments to push for the international isolation of South Africa through diplomatic and economic sanctions against that country. Aside from King and Luthuli, many social activists and religious and world leaders signed the appeal. At that same time, King and his SCLC were launching a major campaign to strike down the entire system of segregation in Albany, Georgia.

King's strategy was to build a coalition of conscience in America while contributing to a larger, worldwide coalition of conscience to challenge racism internationally. He made major speeches on South African apartheid in England in December 1964, while en route to Oslo, Norway, to receive the Nobel Peace Prize, and at Hunter College in New York in December 1965. In the 1964 speech, King highlighted the need for the release of imprisoned black South African leaders such as Nelson Mandela and Robert Sobukwe, and challenged the world community, especially the United States and England, to withdraw all economic support for the South African regime, including the purchase of gold. Unfortunately, King's statements on the white-supremacist policies and practices of the South African government at that time received little or no attention from major media sources in America and Europe. Those statements are still virtually ignored even by the most reputable King scholars.

In the 1965 speech, delivered after King and his coalition of conscience had spearheaded a successful voting rights campaign in Selma, Alabama, King reiterated the call for economic sanctions against South Africa and declared that "the potent non-violent path" that had brought racial change in the United States and liberation to India and regions in Africa should be employed on a more global scale to defeat the forces of racism in South Africa and globally. The failure to respond creatively and constructively to racism as a world problem, said King in one of his last books, *Where Do We Go from Here: Chaos or Community?* (1967), could only lead to a race war and perhaps the fall of Western civilization. Interestingly enough, King's call for economic sanctions would be echoed repeatedly in the 1980s, twenty years later, as the world grew less and less tolerant of the South African apartheid system.

In recent years, the United Nations has held a number of international conferences on racism, and this should also be a reminder of the timelessness of certain concerns that King raised around that issue. King recognized in his own time that the dialogue on race necessarily had to be reframed, far beyond but not neglecting black-white relations in the United States, and this need continues today. Predictions of the emergence of a postracial America (and world) after the election of President Barack Obama have proven premature, and some scholars are now writing about the globalization of racism. King wrote of this phenomenon years ago, and his prescience and the continuing relevance of his insights need to be appreciated and better understood. (See the documents included in part II entitled "Confronting the Color Bar: Overcoming Racism as a World Problem.")

King often said that global racism and colonialism are almost synonymous, or "legitimate first cousins," for both involve levels of political control, economic exploitation, cultural imperialism, and the debasement of human personality. As King studied the history of Western colonialism and its subjugation of Africans, Asians, and other peoples of color, from the late fifteenth to the twentieth centuries, he saw the worst aspects of the European-American temperament in magnified form. He also witnessed the immeasurable psychological impact of both colonialism and neocolonialism on their victims. Although King lived to see the death of colonialism in much of the world, he was disturbed by the developing trends in neocolonialism, which was practiced through economic arrangements that allowed the former colonial powers to exploit their former colonies.

The enduring threat that the various expressions of colonialism posed to the creation of world community remained uppermost in King's thinking, particularly as he considered what would inevitably be their tragic legacy. For King, much of that legacy was evident in the manner in which the governments and political leaders of the former colonies in Africa, Asia, and Latin America exploited their subjects, while amassing wealth and living in luxury themselves. Thus, King said and wrote a great deal about the need to wipe out not only the last vestiges of colonialism but also the colonized mentality. King also made his attack on these evils a part of his overall struggle to eliminate global racism. Given his concept of "the interrelated structure of all reality," he was always apt to see these problems as manifestations of the same global structures of oppression and victimization. (See part III, "Breaking the Chains of Colonialism: The Rise of Peoples of Color in the Third World.")

King felt that the assault on world racism and colonialism could not be successfully made without an equally powerful attack on poverty and economic injustice as international problems. From the time of the Montgomery bus boycott, which clearly had economic repercussions, King spoke of racism and economic injustice as perennial allies, but his most persistent, organized attack on the problems emerged in the mid- and late 1960s. King led a nonviolent army against economic inequality and discrimination in real estate in Chicago in 1965 and 1966, and Eugene Carson Blake and others in the National and World Council of Churches felt that the Chicago Freedom Movement might provide a model for attacking poverty on the international level. King and his SCLC continued the assault by organizing a Poor People's Campaign in 1967 and by participating in a strike of sanitation workers in Memphis, Tennessee, in early 1968.

But King realized that blacks in America were not the only victims of poverty in the world. This mindset helps us understand his plan to intersect blacks, poor whites, Mexicans, Native Americans, and other racial and ethnic groups in the Poor People's Campaign, a campaign he would not live to lead. This also accounted for his financial and moral support for liberation movements worldwide, and his devotion to an analysis of world poverty in his last two books, *Where Do We Go from Here: Chaos or Community?* (1967) and *The Trumpet of Conscience* (1968). King's insights into and analysis of world poverty, as well as his recommendations for attacking and eliminating the problem, still rank among the most penetrating and sophisticated on record.

King pointed out that two-thirds of the world lived in grinding poverty, a problem that inevitably led to undernourishment, malnutrition, homelessness, the lack of health care, disease, and death. As King saw it, the population explosion merely exacerbated the problem. King called for "a radical redistribution" of the world's economic and material resources to feed the unfed, to clothe the naked, to house the homeless, and to heal the sick. This all-out war against world poverty would also include, in his estimation, a sort of foreign-aid program by which America, Canada, and wealthy nations in Western Europe would provide capital and technical assistance for underdeveloped countries. Mindful of how the Western powers had long exploited poor nations through systems of colonialism and neocolonialism, King insisted that foreign aid be provided out of a sense of moral obligation and not as just another gimmick for controlling poor and underdeveloped countries in Africa, Asia, Latin America, and the Caribbean.

Almost a half century after King's death, poverty and economic injustice are still the close companions of racism, and the gap that separates what King called the haves from the have-nots of the world has grown wider. The United Nations' world food programs and foreign aid from wealthy nations have done little to end the problem. "The least of these" can still be found in every nation, including the United States and Western Europe. Coalitions of conscience that fight against poverty and economic exploitation, based on the model provided by King and the SCLC in the Poor People's Campaign, are virtually nonexistent. Furthermore, the bankruptcy of the global economy is increasingly in the realm of the possibility. In such a world climate, there is still much to be learned from King about how individuals, social groups, and nations might work together to ensure that people everywhere have adequate material resources and the basic necessities of life. (See documents in part IV, "For the Least of These: Launching the Global War on Poverty.")

The same might be said of war and human destruction. As far back as the 1950s, King opposed war on moral and pragmatic grounds and, by the early 1960s, had signed numerous statements with other liberal Americans condemning it as "the most colossal" of all social evils. After receiving the Nobel Peace Prize in 1964, and to some extent before that time, King dismissed war as obsolete, maintaining that all violence was ultimately irrational, immoral, and self-defeating. He used the Vietnam conflict to drive home his point about the evils of war, pointing especially to the unnecessary slaughter of the Vietnamese people and the destruction of their homes, places of worship, and rice fields. From 1965 until his assassination in 1968, King consistently denounced what he termed America's misadventure in Vietnam in the pulpits of churches and during peace demonstrations in the streets of America. King felt that it was his moral duty as a prophet and as "a citizen of the world" to do so. His most celebrated speech on the subject, "Beyond Vietnam: A Time to Break Silence," was delivered at the historic Riverside Church in New York City on April 4, 1967, exactly a year before his murder.

In the late 1960s, King also turned once again to a coalition of conscience, Clergy and Laity Concerned About Vietnam (CALC), an organization of socially active religious leaders, to more effectively address the Vietnam conflict and the problem of war generally. King saw religious leaders as the chief voices of morality and peace in the challenge to the U.S. involvement in Vietnam, and he made this abundantly clear in his commentary, "Peace: God's Man's Business," which appeared in the January 1–7, 1966, issue of the *Chicago Defender*. Some of King's most powerful addresses on war were printed and circulated through CALC in the late sixties, among which were "The Casualties of the War in Vietnam" and "Beyond Vietnam: A Time to Break Silence," both of which appear in this volume.

King's antiwar witness and crusade are desperately needed in a contemporary world in which war is still too often glorified, and in which humans are haunted by sectarian warfare in Iraq, organized torture and terrorism, ethnic cleansings, genocide, religiously based violence, political assassinations, and the cycles of violence, repression, and reprisal in the Middle East. No one recalls King's suggestion that "the arms race" be replaced by "the peace race," and the United Nations, which King saw as a giant step in the direction of nonviolence on an international scale, seems distressingly inadequate as the world's peacemaking and peacekeeping force. King once observed, in a moment of stern prophecy, that humanity must put an end to war or war will put an end to humanity. These words still represent the voice of reason in the midst of human folly. King's suggestion that nations move beyond an intellectual analysis of nonviolence to a practical application of this method in their relations with each other may seem politically naïve, but it is morally sound.

For those who honor King's legacy, the struggle today should be geared toward a culture of peace that goes beyond international conflict to address conflict between individuals and groups. King knew that criminal violence, psychological violence, domestic violence, and other types of violence, when considered jointly, could possibly pose as much of a threat to world community and peace as war. Pedophilia, sexism, and homophobia have become metaphors for violence between individuals and groups today. Thus, we are compelled also to revisit King's call for nonviolence in interpersonal and intergroup relations. (Documents on war and peace issues, which reveal the maturation of King's nonviolent ethic over time, comprise part V, "To Study War No More: An Affirmation of World Peace and Human Coexistence.")

In setting forth his vision of living in "the world house," King did not ignore the need to address religious bigotry and intolerance. He called for a fresh ecumenical and interfaith spirit, or for a spirit of mutual respect, understanding, dialogue, and cooperation between Christians, Jews, Hindus, Buddhists, Muslims, and peoples of other faith traditions. King marched, sang, and prayed with Protestants, Catholics, and Jews in civil rights campaigns in the United States; he united with Hindus, Buddhists, Muslims, African traditionalists, and people of other faiths in putting forth and signing appeals and declarations against racial oppression, poverty and economic exploitation, and wars of aggression. King also signed statements lamenting the treatment of Jews in Russia and of Christians and other people of faith in a number of Communist countries. Indeed, he left a glowing legacy of respect for other religions, ideologies, and cultures, seeing in them tremendous possibilities for learning and personal growth.

Religious bigotry and intolerance accounts for the anti-Islamic, anti-Arab sensibilities in much of our society today, and this is leading to increasing attacks against Muslims and their institutions. The problem is indeed worldwide, often exploding in violence between Jews and Muslims in the Middle East, Hindus and Christians in India, Hindus and Muslims in Pakistan, and different factions of Muslims in Iraq. King's insistence that all people of faith are children of God, and that there is more truth in all religions combined than in any one religion, is food for thought in this world of religious conflict. He understood that religious conflict would remain inevitable as long as some in the world's faith communities parade as if they have a monopoly on truth. (See the documents on religious pluralism, interfaith co-operation, and King's collaborative efforts with leaders of various faith traditions in part VI, "Toward a Positive Pluralism: Interfaith Dialogue and Global Community.")

Significantly, King saw "the new world order" coming into being in his lifetime, but he also understood that there were still barriers that had to be transcended before this ideal could find full realization. King wrote and said a lot about both the external (i.e., racism, poverty and economic injustice, war, religious bigotry and intolerance) and internal barriers (i.e., fear, ignorance, greed, hatred) to world community and peace, and, as noted earlier, he highlighted the importance of worldwide coalitions of conscience in striking down such barriers.

The material here extends from 1954 to 1968 and illustrates how King's world vision expanded and matured over time, resulting in a more enlightened and explicit globalism. I trust this book will lead to a new appreciation for the global King and his relevance in the emergence and shaping of the modern world. *"In a Single Garment of Destiny"* shows King's influence on liberation struggles worldwide and proves that he continues to inform what it means to live, to be human, and to relate to others in this pluralistic world.

PART I

All of God's Children:
Toward a Global Vision
of Human Liberation

*I am absolutely convinced that God is not interested
merely in the freedom of black men and brown men and
yellow men. But God is interested in the freedom of the
whole human race, the creation of a society where all
men will live together as brothers and every man will
respect the dignity and worth of all human personality.*

— "The Three Dimensions of a Complete Life," a sermon
delivered at the Unitarian Church of Germantown,
Philadelphia, Pennsylvania, December 11, 1960

Introduction

Martin Luther King, Jr., viewed the world as a vast and complex mosaic that demanded sweeping, transformative change in order to survive. He used metaphors such as "the world house," "the worldwide neighborhood," "the human family," and "the beloved community" in articulating his vision of an inter-related and interdependent world in which people recognize bonds and obligations among themselves. The three documents in part I testify to King's unwavering love for humanity, to his broad and inclusive vision of human community, and to his practical quest for what he termed "a new world order." These documents also help explain why King is being increasingly associated today with a globalized rights culture.

"The Vision of a World Made New," dated September 9, 1954, is included here because it is one of King's earliest and most important speeches on "the dying old and the emerging new" global order. The speech is provided in its entirety for several reasons. First, because it clearly challenges the view, promoted even by some King scholars, that King had no clearly defined and sophisticated world vision prior to receiving the Nobel Peace Prize in December 1964. Second, the speech proves that King, who had only recently become pastor of the Dexter Avenue Baptist Church in Montgomery, Alabama, was highly sensitive to the interplay of systems of oppression worldwide based on race and economics, even before he made his first attempt at organized social protest. He had become fully convinced that the struggles of people in Africa and Asia against Western imperialism and colonialism could not be separated from his own people's plight under Jim Crow in the southern United States. Finally, the speech yields important insights into what constituted the ideal world for the twenty-five-year-old King.

"The World House," prepared in 1967 as part of the last chapter in King's book *Where Do We Go from Here: Chaos or Community?* was written some thirteen years later. One is exposed here to a more mature King, who had apparently moved toward a more enlightened and explicit globalism. This would not have been surprising because, by this time, King had read widely, traveled the world over, and observed the vast landscape of humanity. Moreover, the Nobel Prize had given him a mandate to address international issues and concerns with greater urgency, and so he focused in "The World House" on "the scientific and technological revolutions" that essentially made all peoples neighbors, on the rising tide of global liberation movements among the oppressed, and on what it means for people to live creatively and harmoniously. King also highlighted the relationship between the black freedom crusade in America and the efforts to end the systems of domination and exploitation in other nations, an issue that consistently surfaces in his speeches, sermons, addresses, letters, and interviews in the period from 1954 up to his death fourteen years later.

In his address to the European Baptist Assembly in Amsterdam, Holland, entitled "Revolution and Redemption" and dated August 16, 1964, King reminded Christians everywhere that they were "living in a world of revolution," scientifically, technologically, and in terms of the struggle for human freedom and community, and he explained what this meant for those who proclaimed the true gospel of Jesus Christ. In King's mind, "the work of missionaries around the world" consisted not so much in saving souls, as many fundamentalists and evangelicals in his day argued, but in saving humanity. Evidently, King moved beyond the idea of foreign missions as proselytizing ventures to foreign missions as service to humanity. The central idea coursing through "Revolution and Redemption" is that the followers of Jesus Christ must become a greater force not in Christianizing the world but in humanizing the world.

Considered jointly, the documents in this first part of *"In a Single Garment of Destiny"* highlight the need to forge a new conception of humanity and the world. They speak to the need for a globally responsible ethic of human existence and cooperation, which was the basis of the universality of King's concern for humanity. In an increasingly globalized world of plurality and difference, King, unlike many Americans in his own time and even today, understood the danger inherent in the Manichean division of the world into us and them. King hoped that people everywhere would, in the midst of the tension and uncertainty of the changing times, reaffirm their ties to each other.

But King also knew that this would require a revolution of values and priorities, a consideration taken into account in all of the documents in part I. Thus, he insisted that every person, and especially children and youth, should develop "a world perspective." King also spoke of the pressing need to move beyond "a thing-oriented society" to "a person-oriented society" and from the belief that "self-preservation is the first law of life" to an affirmation that "other preservation is the first law of life." He felt that flesh-and-blood human beings had to become more precious than the material things of life and that an altruistic ethic, or an unselfish concern for others, had to replace the human tendency toward egoism and selfishness. Furthermore, King held that his own native land, the United States, due to its technology and vast resources, should assume a more positive and creative role, indeed a leadership role, in this values-driven quest for "a new humanity" and "a new world order." At the same time, he understood that, in such a world, his own country had as much to learn as it had to teach.

People have not yet evolved into the kind of interconnected global society that King envisioned and sought to achieve. The documents in part I suggest that as long as there is a quest for such a society, King is meaningful and relevant. The documents are important not merely because they reveal King's affinity to common humanity, his interest in advancing universal human rights, his call for a new era of engagement with the world, and how he sought to eliminate the intractable moral, social, and political problems that afflicted the human family but also because they answer many timeless questions about what it means to be truly human in relation to other human beings. These documents are as well a resource for a radical critique of any worldview that casually embraces and sanctions the world and human life as they are.

"The Vision of a World Made New"

Speech by Martin Luther King, Jr.

Annual Meeting of the Women's Convention Auxiliary
National Baptist Convention

ST. LOUIS, MISSOURI, SEPTEMBER 9, 1954

Frequently there appears on the stage of history individuals who have the insight to look beyond the inadequacies of the old order and see the necessity for the new. These are the persons with a sort of divine discontent. They realize that the world as it is is far from the world that it ought to be. They never confuse the "isness" of an old order with the "oughtness" of a new order. And so in every age and every generation there are those persons who have envisioned some new order. Plato envisioned it in his *Republic* as a time when justice would reign throughout society and philosophers would become kings and kings philosophers. Karl Marx envisioned it as the emergence of a classless society in which the proletariat would ultimately conquer the reign of the bourgeoisie. Out of such a vision grew the slogan "From each according to his ability, to each according to his need." Edward Bellamy envisioned it [in] *Looking Backward* as a time when the inequalities of monopoly capitalism would be blotted out and all men would live on a relatively equal plane with all of the conveniences of life. The Christian religion envisioned it as the kingdom of God, a time when God would reign supreme in all life and love, brotherhood and right relationship would be the order of society. In every age men have quested and longed for a new order.

Many centuries ago a man by the name of John was in prison on a lonely, obscure island called Patmos. In such a situation he was deprived of almost every freedom, but the freedom to think.

6

He thought about many things. He thought about a possible new world and a new social order. He meditated on the need for a change in the old pattern of things. So one day he cried out: "I saw a new heaven and a new earth. . . . [*ellipsis in original*] I saw the holy city, new Jerusalem, coming down from God out of heaven."

John could talk meaningfully about the new Jerusalem because he had experienced the old Jerusalem with its perfunctory ceremonialism, its tragic gulfs between abject poverty and inordinate wealth, its political domination and economic exploitation. John could see this old Jerusalem passing away and the new Jerusalem coming into being.

John is saying something quite significant here. He realized that the old earth did not represent the earth as it should be. He knew that the conditions of the old Jerusalem did not represent the permanent structure of the universe. The old Jerusalem represented injustice, crushing domination, and the triumph of the forces of darkness. The new Jerusalem represented justice, brotherhood and the triumph of the forces of light. So when John said he saw the new Jerusalem, he was saying in substance that he saw justice conquering injustice, he saw the forces of darkness consumed by the forces of light. Ultimately history brings into being the new order to blot out the tragic reign of the old order.

II. Now if we will look far enough we will see the truth of John's vision being revealed in the contemporary world. Today we stand between two worlds, a world- that is gradually passing away and a world that is being born. We stand between the dying old and the emerging new.

   A. On a world scale we have seen the old order in the form of colonialism and imperialism. These lead to domination and exploitation.

      (1) Number of persons in the world as compared with number of colored.

      (2) Fifty years ago the vast majority of these persons were under some colonial power.

India under British
Africa under British, French and Dutch
China   "   "   "   "   "
Indonesia under the Dutch

    (3) One of the tragedies of the Church was that it became allied to the old order. Note South Africa and India.

    (4) But in spite of this we have gradually seen the old order pass away. Most of these colonial people are now free.

    (5) So, like John, we can say we see a new heaven and a new earth. The old order of ungodly exploitation and crushing domination is passing away.

B. On a national scale we have seen the old order in the form of segregation and discrimination.

    (1) Segregation has been an instrument all along to remind the Negro of his inferior status. Its presupposition is that the group that is segregated is inferior to the group that is segregating.

    (2) Through segregation the Negro has been dominated politically . . .

    (3) The tragedy is that the Church sanctioned it.

    (4) But the tide has turned now. Segregation is passing away.

III. Notice one other point of the text. It mentions that this new city descends out of heaven from God rather than ascends out of earth from man.

"The World House"

Statement by Martin Luther King, Jr.

From *Where Do We Go from Here:*
Chaos or Community?

1967

Some years ago a famous novelist died. Among his papers was found a list of suggested plots for future stories, the most prominently underscored being this one: "A widely separated family inherits a house in which they have to live together." This is the great new problem of mankind. We have inherited a large house, a great "world house" in which we have to live together—black and white, Easterner and Westerner, Gentile and Jew, Catholic and Protestant, Muslim and Hindu—a family unduly separated in ideas, culture and interest, who, because we can never again live apart, must learn somehow to live with each other in peace.

However deeply American Negroes are caught in the struggle to be at last at home in our homeland of the United States, we cannot ignore the larger world house in which we are also dwellers. Equality with whites will not solve the problems of either whites or Negroes if it means equality in a world society stricken by poverty and in a universe doomed to extinction by war.

All inhabitants of the globe are now neighbors. This worldwide neighborhood has been brought into being largely as a result of the modern scientific and technological revolutions. The world of today is vastly different from the world of just one hundred years ago. A century ago Thomas Edison had not yet invented the incandescent lamp to bring light to many dark places of the earth. The Wright brothers had not yet invented that fascinating mechanical bird that would spread its gigantic wings across the skies and soon dwarf distance and place time in the service of man. Einstein had not yet challenged an axiom and the theory of relativity had not yet been posited.

Human beings, searching a century ago as now for better understanding, had no television, no radios, no telephones and no motion pictures through which to communicate. Medical science had not yet discovered the wonder drugs to end many dread plagues and diseases. One hundred years ago military men had not yet developed the terrifying weapons of warfare that we know today—not the bomber, an airborne fortress raining down death; nor napalm, that burner of all things and flesh in its path. A century ago there were no sky-scraping buildings to kiss the stars and no gargantuan bridges to span the waters. Science had not yet peered into the unfathomable ranges of interstellar space, nor had it penetrated oceanic depths. All these new inventions, these new ideas, these sometimes fascinating and sometimes frightening developments, came later. Most of them have come within the past sixty years, sometimes with agonizing slowness, more characteristically with bewildering speed, but always with enormous significance for our future.

The years ahead will see a continuation of the same dramatic developments. Physical science will carve new highways through the stratosphere. In a few years astronauts and cosmonauts will probably walk comfortably across the uncertain pathways of the moon. In two or three years it will be possible, because of the new supersonic jets, to fly from New York to London in two and one-half hours. In the years ahead medical science will greatly prolong the lives of men by finding a cure for cancer and deadly heart ailments. Automation and cybernation will make it possible for working people to have undreamed-of amounts of leisure time. All this is a dazzling picture of the furniture, the workshop, the spacious rooms, the new decorations and the architectural pattern of the large world house in which we are living.

Along with the scientific and technological revolution, we have also witnessed a worldwide freedom revolution over the last few decades. The present upsurge of the Negro people of the United States grows out of a deep and passionate determination to make freedom and equality a reality "here" and "now." In one sense the civil rights movement in the United States is a special American phenomenon which must be understood in the light of American history and dealt with in terms of the American situation. But on another and more important level, what is happening in the United States today is a significant part of a world development.

We live in a day, said the philosopher Alfred North Whitehead, "when civilization is shifting its basic outlook; a major turning point in history where the pre-suppositions on which society is structured are being analyzed, sharply challenged, and profoundly changed." What we are seeing now is a freedom explosion, the realization of "an idea whose time has come," to use Victor Hugo's phrase. The deep rumbling of discontent that we hear today is the thunder of disinherited masses, rising from dungeons of oppression to the bright hills of freedom. In one majestic chorus the rising masses are singing, in the words of our freedom song, "Ain't gonna let nobody turn us around." All over the world like a fever, freedom is spreading in the widest liberation movement in history. The great masses of people are determined to end the exploitation of their races and lands. They are awake and moving toward their goal like a tidal wave. You can hear them rumbling in every village street, on the docks, in the houses, among the students, in the churches and at political meetings. For several centuries the direction of history flowed from the nations and societies of Western Europe out into the rest of the world in "conquests" of various sorts. That period, the era of colonialism, is at an end. East is moving West. The earth is being redistributed. Yes, we are "shifting our basic outlooks."

These developments should not surprise any student of history. Oppressed people cannot remain oppressed forever. The yearning for freedom eventually manifests itself. The Bible tells the thrilling story of how Moses stood in Pharaoh's court centuries ago and cried, "Let my people go." This was an opening chapter in a continuing story. The present struggle in the United

States is a later chapter in the same story. Something within has reminded the Negro of his birthright of freedom, and something without has reminded him that it can be gained. Consciously or unconsciously, he has been caught up by the spirit of the times, and with his black brothers of Africa and his brown and yellow brothers in Asia, South America and the Caribbean, the United States Negro is moving with a sense of great urgency toward the promised land of racial justice.

Nothing could be more tragic than for men to live in these revolutionary times and fail to achieve the new attitudes and the new mental outlooks that the new situation demands. In Washington Irving's familiar story of Rip Van Winkle, the one thing that we usually remember is that Rip slept twenty years. There is another important point, however, that is almost always overlooked. It was the sign on the inn in the little town on the Hudson from which Rip departed and scaled the mountain for his long sleep. When he went up, the sign had a picture of King George III of England. When he came down, twenty years later, the sign had a picture of George Washington. As he looked at the picture of the first President of the United States, Rip was confused, flustered and lost. He knew not who Washington was. The most striking thing about this story is not that Rip slept twenty years, but that he slept through a revolution that would alter the course of human history.

One of the great liabilities of history is that all too many people fail to remain awake through great periods of social change. Every society has its protectors of the status quo and its fraternities of the indifferent who are notorious for sleeping through revolutions. But today our very survival depends on our ability to stay awake, to adjust to new ideas, to remain vigilant and to face the challenge of change. The large house in which we live demands that we transform this worldwide neighborhood into a worldwide brotherhood. Together we must learn to live as brothers or together we will be forced to perish as fools.

We must work passionately and indefatigably to bridge the gulf between our scientific progress and our moral progress. One of the great problems of mankind is that we suffer from a poverty of the spirit which stands in glaring contrast to our scientific and technological abundance. The richer we have become materially, the poorer we have become morally and spiritually.

Every man lives in two realms, the internal and the external. The internal is that realm of spiritual ends expressed in art, literature, morals and religion. The external is that complex of devices, techniques, mechanisms and instrumentalities by means of which we live. Our problem today is that we have allowed the internal to become lost in the external. We have allowed the means by which we live to outdistance the ends for which we live. So much of modern life can be summarized in that suggestive phrase of Thoreau: "Improved means to an unimproved end." This is the serious predicament, the deep and haunting problem, confronting modern man. Enlarged material powers spell enlarged peril if there is not proportionate growth of the soul. When the external of man's nature subjugates the internal, dark storm clouds begin to form.

Western civilization is particularly vulnerable at this moment, for our material abundance has brought us neither peace of mind nor serenity of spirit. An Asian writer has portrayed our dilemma in candid terms:

> You call your thousand material devices "labor-saving machinery," yet you are forever "busy." With the multiplying of your machinery you grow increasingly fatigued, anxious, nervous, dissatisfied. Whatever you have, you want more; and wherever you are you want to go somewhere else . . . your devices are neither time-saving nor soul-saving machinery. They are so many sharp spurs which urge you on to invent more machinery and to do more business.

This tells us something about our civilization that cannot be cast aside as a prejudiced charge by an Eastern thinker who is jealous of Western prosperity. We cannot escape the indictment.

This does not mean that we must turn back the clock of scientific progress. No one can overlook the wonders that science has wrought for our lives. The automobile will not abdicate in favor of the horse and buggy, or the train in favor of the stagecoach, or the tractor in favor of the hand plow, or the scientific method in favor of ignorance and superstition. But our moral and spiritual "lag" must be redeemed. When scientific power outruns moral power, we end up with guided missiles and misguided men. When we foolishly minimize the internal of our lives and maximize the external, we sign the warrant for our own day of doom.

Our hope for creative living in this world house that we have inherited lies in our ability to reestablish the moral ends of our lives in personal character and social justice. Without this spiritual and moral reawakening we shall destroy ourselves in the misuse of our own instruments.

"Revolution and Redemption"

Address by Martin Luther King, Jr.

European Baptist Assembly

AMSTERDAM, HOLLAND, AUGUST 16, 1964

———◇◇◇———

It is indeed a pleasure to meet with fellow Baptists from all over Europe and the world. And it is a special privilege for me to share with this Christian body some of the concerns which the Gospel of Jesus Christ brings to the hearts of men in these times of revolution and change.

The gospel message is sharper than a two edged sword, but little did we realize just how sharp when we began to share this message with the nations of the non-Western world. Little was this realized when the slave masters of the United States began to read the Bible to the house servants and encourage them to preach to the others. The fact that we are living in a world of revolution is in a large measure attributable to the preaching of the Gospel, and the work of missionaries around the world.

Now we have a world in turmoil, but we must remember that the turmoil is in part due to the preaching of God's Word and to the belief of the brethren.

It was Christian preaching that first spread the idea of the Brotherhood of all mankind throughout the world. It was Christian preaching that gave men and nations something in which to hope. It was Christian preaching that began the movement of education for all. It was finally Christian preaching that convinced men that the evils of the world might be overcome, and that these nations of the West, under Christ, would lead them into a new earthly Kingdom where men might live together as in the Kingdom of God. They heard our promise and took it literally. Now they are demanding that the promise of the Kingdom be fulfilled here and now.

15

We now realize that much of this was based on an unbiblical theology and that in our own enthusiasm to bring the world to Christ we allowed our faith in Christ and our faith in Western culture and technology to become interchanged, but this does not relieve us of responsibility for our preaching.

Now many Christians have forgotten our involvement in the beginnings of this revolution and see only a mass of humanity shouting Freedom. They have forgotten or denied their involvement in the beginnings of this world revolution. They have allowed the Communist to take full credit for the revolutionary state in which the world finds itself. Western Christians have too long been identified with [a] comfortable stable existence to adapt readily to a world of change. Yet this is just what God requires of us in these times. We must not forsake our earlier efforts to bring the World to Christ merely because it does not come to Christ as we imagined it would.

There are two aspects of the world which we must never forget. One is that this is God's world, and He is active in the forces of history and the affairs of men. The second is, that Jesus Christ gave his life for the redemption of this world, and as his followers, we are called to give our lives continuing the reconciling work of Christ in *this* world.

Let us look for a moment at the nature of the revolutions of our time. We may discern more of the hand of God moving amongst them than we have heretofore realized.

At the bottom of every revolution is the dawning of the idea that all men are created equal. In the Southern Freedom Movement of the United States, we say that the movement begins when men and women realize that they are children of God. If we are all really God's children, then all of us are entitled to the same opportunities, pleasures, and responsibilities. This is the seed from which all the aspirations of humanity grow.

This aspiration is so widespread that it assumes national proportions in our time. Not only do individuals want to take their places alongside other men, but we are engaged in a struggle of nations, each fighting for her own national place in the sun. Any force which seems to stand in the way of this drive is destined to be overturned.

The means through which mankind has decided to gain equality is human ingenuity, better known as technology. The resources of men's minds and the machines of their creation now seek to build a world where every man might share in the bounties and rewards which in former times were only available to the rich.

What this means is that man is now truly a partner with God in the continuation of his creation. No longer does he wait and pray for some supernatural power to deliver him from his misery; he has marshaled his talents and organized his skills and anxiously proceeds to build a world to answer his needs and desires.

The emergence of technological man has led him to create for himself huge metropolitan complexes. Our entire way of life has changed within this generation. The move to the city is the most widespread phenomenon in the world today. Minority groups and nations may cry freedom, but men of every nation, rich or poor; black, white or in between; now move to the city in an unexpressed search for freedom from want, deprivation and the simple village life of their fathers.

The total impact of these and other forces is a world in motion. Just where the world is moving is an open question. But there can be no denial of the fact that the whole creation is anxiously seeking some sort of fulfillment.

The immediate temptation for the church is to attempt to call the world back to more stable times; to admonish our congregations not to forsake the ways of their fathers. But to do this is to forget the God who promises to "make all things new"[1] and whose plan it is for the fullness of time "to unite all things in Him, things in Heaven and things on earth."[2] Our calling is much more difficult and hazardous, for again God calls us as he did

---

1. Revelation 21:3
2. Ephesians 1:10

Abraham to venture into a land which we know not. He calls us to live with Christ in the midst of a world in revolution.

Admittedly, we are no more prepared to enter this world than was Abraham to venture out into the desert, but there is no choice for us at this point, for to remain in a secure 18th century existence while the world moves on, will certainly mean the death of the church, and without the prophetic witness of the church, the entire world may become one great holocaust.

Indeed, we see the evidence of this already. The church has remained silent these past years and allowed the world to go on unattended, and we are witnessing the gradual corrosion of both church and world before our very eyes. Here in Europe, the decline of church attendance makes this fact obvious; but in the United States, the same thing is true. What we are witnessing there is a last desperate rush to the church in hopes that Mother Church might defend us from the insecurities of this age and keep us safe in her bosom for the age to come. But in spite of the masses who gather each Sunday, there is the constant deterioration of community and family life and the corruption of our national life as evidenced by the popularity of a presidential candidate who promises to return the nation to a world of the past, where there will be no taxes, no foreign aid, no social security, and no problems that can't be solved by nuclear power. And the very people who are making this candidate so popular are the people who fill our churches in the midwestern and southern states.

The alternative to escape is a creative and courageous attempt to enter the world in revolution and there struggle with the principalities and powers of this age as though we really believed that Christ has overcome the world, not just our little private world of salvation for my own soul, but the world of rockets, steel mills, and hungry over-populated nations.

Negro Christians are in many ways fortunate. We have no choice. There can be no escape. We must trust God and live the life he has placed before us. Necessity has forced us to cling to

Him in faith. When we were in slavery and had no money, no education, no worldly power whatsoever, we learned that we could sing of Sweet Chariots which would come and carry us home when the burden got too heavy. We learned that Jeremiah's question does have an answer and that there is a "balm in Gilead, to heal the sin sick soul." We learned that in the darkest hours of frustration and despair God will make a way. And so we know of God's power in ways that are as real to us as the forces of this revolutionary world. Therefore it was not hard for us to believe the theme song of our movement, "We Shall Overcome."

It was difficult however to move from the private spheres of faith into the public and social orbit. For many years American Negroes sought to overcome the evils and temptations of society through individual acts of faith and worship. This offered very little hope. It did teach us that we must work together, seek together and suffer together if we are to overcome the powers which enslave us.

It was Montgomery, Alabama, that God chose to teach us this lesson. God took a simple incident of a woman being mistreated on a public bus to teach the Negroes of Montgomery and the entire United States, of the power of group action and witness. From this humble beginning, he has led us and taught us many things about the organization and mobilization of love and goodwill into a powerful action movement, which is capable of coping with the tremendous forces of this age.

In Birmingham, Alabama, we saw this movement come to fruition, and witnessed the entire wheels of a nation turn to cope with the problem of racial justice. The organization in Love of three thousand citizens brought about the most sweeping legislation on the question of race and color that this nation has known since the signing of the Emancipation Proclamation.

What we have learned from this is that the individual faith, hope and charity of our congregations must be mobilized into group witness, if we are to make any impact on the conscience of our world. We have an expression that "anything ten thousand people in the United States become convinced of and are willing to suffer for can become a reality." The freedom movement so far has borne this out as fact.

I say this to you, because race is not the only issue which confronts our world, and Negroes are not the only Christians who are in need of justice. It is time that the methods of organized goodwill, or Truth Force, as Gandhi would have called it, become applied to the questions which confront the church in every area of life.

For example, our New Testament charges us to be concerned about the hungry, those in prison . . . [*ellipsis in original*] the least of these our brethren. In an age of revolution, this is exactly what the masses of men and women are asking for, that we do something for those poverty stricken millions who inhabit the under-developed nations of the world.

In a mass technological society, it is not enough to send missionary baskets. It is not even enough to build schools and hospitals. If the millions are to be fed, clothed and housed, the resources of the nations must be put to the task. Mammoth programs of area development, comparable to the Marshall Plan, which aided in the rebuilding of Europe, must be developed to aid Africa and Asia. Christians must encourage, yea demand that their governments act as though the financial and technical resources entrusted to them belong to God, and that these resources are used to the Glory of God for the care of God's children wherever they may be in need.

This is the road evangelism must take in these times. Nations have identified Christianity with the West, and while we must fight this identification, we must also accept responsibility for the governments which we elect, or allow to be elected through our indifference. A Christian might well find himself fighting for a dam or hydro-electric power unit for an under-developed nation, because he realized that this is the key to opening the resources of a nation to the extent that it can provide a modest life for its population. Feeding the hungry and clothing the naked is a complex business in our time, but nevertheless it must be done, and God has called us as his children to see to it that it is done.

In the near future the Church must find some way to direct her concern toward the question of world peace. This is the World for which Christ died. We cannot sit idly by and watch it destroyed by a group of insecure and ambitious egotists who can't see beyond their own designs for power. We are now in a delicate balance of power which results in a condition most near to peace than any we have known for the past twenty-five years. Now is the time for Christians to develop a creative approach to this problem and break the stalemate on disarmament and bring about a thaw in the cold war before it becomes a hot war.

We have heard of the offer of the Vatican to act as a mediator in international disputes. This concern is to be commended, yet one must hasten to say that all Christians have lost the right to serve as reconciling agents in international disputes because of our inaction and cautious strategies in the midst of two past world conflicts. The Church must first discern what God is calling Christians to do in the presence of international conflict, and make this witness known, not merely through pronouncements but by the submission of their bodies as living witness to the truth of Christ. This means both personal bodies and institutional bodies must be willing to bear the burden of the cross. Whole churches may be crucified, but it is our faith that God's way of change is through resurrection, and there can be no resurrection without crucifixion.

PART II

Confronting the Color Bar:
Overcoming Racism as a World Problem

I think we have to honestly admit that the problems in
the world today, as they relate to the question of race,
must be blamed on the whole doctrine of white supremacy,
the whole doctrine of racism, and these doctrines came
into being through the white race and the exploitation
of the colored peoples of the world. . . . Now if the white
world does not recognize this and does not adjust to what
is to be, then we can end up in the world with a kind of
race war, so it depends on the spirit and the readjusting
qualities of the white people of the world, and this will
avoid the kind of violent confrontation between the races
if it is done properly by the white people.

— "Doubts and Certainties: Interview with Martin
　 Luther King, Jr.," February 1968, London, England,
　 interview aired on the BBC, April 4, 1968

Introduction

The problem of racism figured prominently in Martin Luther King, Jr.'s analysis of the world's great social evils. King maintained that racism extended across geographical and cultural boundaries, and he was particularly concerned about racism in the form of white supremacy. Much of what he said and wrote about the problem targeted the United States and the Union of South Africa, which he labeled "classic examples" of organized and institutionalized racism. Although prone to speak of the similarities between the racial situations in the two countries, King concluded that South Africa was by far "the most stubborn and rugged place in the world in the area of race relations." In the seven documents in part II of this book, King emerges as a seasoned thinker and activist who understood the pervasive impact of racism on the institutional structures, ideologies, and practices of Western societies, who spoke vibrantly to people of all races, who dominated much of global consciousness around racial issues in his time, and who consistently highlighted the need to move beyond the white-black binary that had too long framed the conversation on race.

Part II of *"In a Single Garment of Destiny"* brings together a range of King documents, among which are statements, speeches, a carefully worded comment, and a letter. Two of the statements, the Declaration of Conscience (1957) and the Appeal for Action Against Apartheid (1962), are actually worldwide appeals that speak to King's collaborative efforts with other national and world leaders in attacking racism. These appeals also reveal something quite profound about the global King, who not only denounced racism with words but also took practical action to eradicate it. Collaborating with others in the antiracism cause was part of King's practical quest in bringing the principle of the beloved community to vivid life. Through such actions, he was actually mirroring the ever-growing global nature of human life.

The Declaration of Conscience was drafted under the auspices of the American Committee on Africa (ACOA), a New York–based organization of pacifists, originally founded in 1951 as Americans for South African Resistance (AFSAR) and devoted to African liberation causes. King's name appeared on the documents of the ACOA as early as 1957, and he was among the initial sponsors of the Declaration, along with the former first lady Eleanor Roosevelt and the Episcopal bishop James A. Pike. Roosevelt served as international chairman of the effort, Pike as U.S. chairman, and King as U.S. vice chairman. The Declaration underscored the "organized inhumanity" and oppressive character of South African apartheid, deemed it a serious threat to world community, and called for cooperative action in uprooting it. King wrote and signed letters promoting the initiative. An estimated 123 heads of state, religious leaders, and academics from various countries, inspired largely by King's involvement, signed the Declaration. From that point, the South African government included King among its greatest enemies in the United States, denouncing him as a communist and rabble-rouser. Also, King was isolated as a source of influence in South Africa, and any South African who read his works or listened to his speeches faced the charge of maintaining "subversive ties."

This image of King was reinforced in the white South African mind when he became the cosponsor, with the black South African leader Albert J. Luthuli, of the Appeal for Action Against Apartheid (1962), another document in part II. Luthuli was a Methodist lay preacher and head of the African National Congress (ANC), an organization that had embraced pragmatic nonviolence since its founding in 1912, and he and King had previously exchanged letters around human rights concerns. Both promoted the Appeal through statements and letters, with a particular emphasis on the need for protest meetings and demonstrations, economic and diplomatic sanctions against the South African regime, and the international isolation of South Africa. The effort was actually "in the nature of a follow-up" to the 1957 Declaration of Conscience and was heavily supported by both the

ACOA and the American Negro Leadership Conference on Africa (ANLCA), an organization started by King and other civil rights leaders in New York in 1962. Roughly 150 world leaders, activists, intellectuals, and representatives of various faith traditions signed the Appeal. King and Luthuli's involvement was highly symbolic of the relationship between the civil rights movement in the United States and the South African anti-apartheid struggle, and it was consistent with King's conviction regarding special bonds and obligations between people of African descent everywhere. Interestingly enough, Luthuli received the Nobel Peace Prize in 1961 and King in 1964, and these recognitions were seen by both as an international endorsement of their crusades against bigotry and intolerance.

King's two major speeches on South African apartheid are among the other documents included in part II. His speech "South African Independence," dated December 7, 1964, was delivered in London, in the presence of blacks from the United States, the Caribbean, and various parts of the African continent. The speech described South Africa's racism as the worst in the world, in part because it even denied blacks the basic right of nonviolent protest, and there was no natural rights tradition even for whites. King also alluded to "the dangers of a race war," recommended economic pressure against South Africa, and suggested that black anti-apartheid activists such as Nelson Mandela of the ANC and Robert Sobukwe of the Pan African Congress should be released from Robben Island Prison.

"Let My People Go" is King's second major speech on South Africa. The title was taken from King's reading of the Biblical Exodus, a Negro spiritual, and Albert J. Luthuli's autobiography, published in 1962. Given at Hunter College in New York on December 10, 1965, Human Rights Day, the speech outlined the evils of racial apartheid while repeating the call for an international boycott of South African goods, a call echoed in many circles worldwide in the 1980s. This was King's longest and most detailed speech on South Africa, a speech punctuated by his calls for "an international alliance" of people against racist policies and practices. Evidently, King had an enduring concern for the global implication of South African apartheid and thought that the rhetoric of mutual alliances and responsibility had to be seriously employed.

King's letter to the South African Embassy, dated February 9, 1966, was selected for part II because it proves King's desire to not only address racial apartheid in sermons, speeches, letters, appeals, petitions, and declarations but also to visit South Africa to discuss human rights concerns with religious leaders, professors, students, and any government officials who would listen to him. In the mid- to late 1960s, King exchanged letters with professors in South African universities and with student groups such as the Anglican Students' Federation (ASF) and the National Union of South African Students (NUSAS) at the University of Cape Town. He was offered lectureships at South African universities through these groups, but the South African Embassy, in a letter dated March 17, 1966, denied King's application for a visa for obvious reasons. Had King visited South Africa, his impact on the anti-apartheid struggle and on racism as a larger global problem would have undoubtedly been far more pervasive and decisive.

King's comment "On the World Taking a Stand on Rhodesia," made on October 25, 1965, is included in part II because it further reveals his fears regarding the impact of white supremacist rule throughout southern Africa. King saw in Rhodesia the potential for another South Africa. He urged the United Nations to back the British government in granting full independence to Southern Rhodesia with a "one-man-one-vote" policy. A black African majority government assumed power in Southern Rhodesia in 1980, twelve years after King's death, and the country was renamed Zimbabwe. This move toward black African majority rule was clearly in line with King's African dream but not the policy of Africanization that has defined Zimbabwe in more recent times, leading to what some human rights theorists deem to be the persecution of white landowners and the confiscation of their properties.

The final document in part II is King's statement "Racism and the World House." This title comes from one of King's last books, 1967's *Where Do We Go from Here: Chaos or Community?* and it serves as a great climax to this section. Here King provided perhaps his most sophisticated analysis of racism as a global phenomenon, with a special focus on both its tragic impact on people of color and its threat to human welfare and survival as a whole. King's essential point was that "the world house" at its best could never be sustained on a foundation of personal and institutionalized racism. His image of "the world house" actually provides a model for new kinds of reflection around issues of race even today.

The world in which King lived and traveled embodied many of the same problems that exist today in the area of race relations. Most disturbing are the lingering, antiquated ideas about race and ethnicity, and the personal and institutionalized racism that continues to fragment the social and political landscape on a national and global scale. The phenomenon of racialized others still defines our world on so many levels, as evidenced in recent times by the rise of hate groups, hate crimes, and politically motivated patterns of racial profiling in the United States, the pandering of the Japanese business community to black stereotypes, the violent confrontations between Chinese and African students in Chinese institutions of higher learning, and the tragic realities of genocide and ethnic cleansing in Rwanda, Bosnia, and Darfur. These new color-line issues must be taken seriously and addressed properly if people are to forge new paths toward an authentically multi-racial and multi-ethnic world. There is a need to revisit so much of what King said about race and how freedom-loving people might best dismantle the structures of racism, while also advancing values that solidify rather than fragment our common humanity. King's legacy of ideas and activism can serve as a resource for a radical critique of how race is viewed and institutionalized worldwide today. The documents in part II of this volume expose us to the moral force of his words and suggest the need for a reconsideration of his meaningfulness for our times.

King was ahead of his time in understanding and articulating the challenges posed by global racism, and he left an imprint upon this world that time will not efface. The documents afforded in part II of *"In a Single Garment of Destiny"* substantiate this claim. King reminded people of all races and ethnic backgrounds that nothing could obscure their innate beauty as creatures shaped in God's image, and he called them to the task of healing their racial and ethnic divisions, to affirming their rich interconnectedness, and to honoring their moral responsibility toward one another in an ever-changing world. Moreover, in the case of race relations in our nation and world, King linked the liberation of the victims of racism with the liberation of the racists themselves. In other words, he maintained that racists and the victims of racism could not be liberated without each other. This was the profundity of King's global ideal of community, and it stands as a message of hope to all who still experience alienation and emptiness due to racial and ethnic barriers.

"Declaration of Conscience"

Joint Statement on South African Apartheid by Martin Luther King, Jr., Bishop James A. Pike, and Eleanor Roosevelt

Under the Auspices of the American Committee on Africa (ACOA)

NEW YORK, NEW YORK, JULY 1957

———◇◇◇———

PREAMBLE

FREEDOM in the Union of South Africa is in grave jeopardy. The South African Government has relentlessly over the past few years extended its policy of organized racism—*apartheid*. 156 leaders who have peacefully sought a just society for all, black and white, are now charged with treason and involved in court action. Laws have just been passed making it a crime for white and non-white to pray in the same church or to study in the same school. Outstanding intellectuals are under court charge for addressing a racially-mixed meeting. Africans are being forced from homes they have occupied for many years so that whites can take over their land. The right to vote is being taken away from colored people in the same manner in which Africans were disenfranchised twenty-one years ago. The Bantu Education Act is being vigorously implemented to educate the African for a role no higher than that of servant in the white man's world.

People everywhere who care about freedom can no longer remain silent while justice and reason are being sacrificed by a Government still enjoying friendly relations with democratic nations of the world.

DECLARATION

WE and free peoples everywhere support the overwhelming majority of the South African people, non-white and white, in their struggle for equality. We support them in their dedication to liberty and their determination to achieve basic human rights for all as proclaimed in their "Freedom Charter":

> *"We the people of South Africa, declare for all our country and the world to know—*
>
> That South Africa belongs to all who live in it, black and white, and that no government can justly claim authority unless it is based on the will of all the people;
>
> That our people have been robbed of their birthright to land, liberty and peace by a form of government founded on injustice and inequality;
>
> That our country will never be prosperous or free until all our people live in brotherhood, enjoying equal rights and opportunities;
>
> That only a democratic state, based on the will of all the people, can secure to all their birthright without distinction of colour, race, sex or belief;
>
> And therefore, we, the people of South Africa, black and white together—equals, countrymen, and brothers— adopt this Freedom Charter. And we pledge ourselves to strive together, sparing nothing of our strength and courage, until democratic changes . . . have been won."

We call on all who are devoted to the principles embodied in the Declaration of Human Rights to join with us in supporting this Declaration of Conscience and in proclaiming December 10, 1957, Human Rights Day, as a Day of Protest against the organized inhumanity of the South African Government and its *apartheid* policies. We call upon free men and women throughout the world to appeal on this day to the Government of the Union of South Africa to observe its moral and legal obligations as a signatory to the United Nations Charter. We call upon men and women everywhere to concentrate their moral and spiritual forces in a universal effort—through prayer, public meetings, and all other peaceful means—on December 10, 1957. We call upon all members of free associations including churches, trade unions, fraternal societies, business, professional, veterans, and other groups to petition their governments and their organizations to mobilize their influence in bringing about a peaceful, democratic and just solution in South Africa. We seek to demonstrate to the Government of South Africa that free men will not tolerate the suppression of freedom. We seek to persuade the South African Government, before it reaches the point of no return, that only in democratic equality is there peace and security.

"Appeal for Action Against Apartheid"

Joint Statement on South African Apartheid by Martin Luther King, Jr., and Chief Albert John Luthuli

Under the Auspices of the American Committee on Africa (ACOA)

JULY 1962

In 1957, an unprecedented Declaration of Conscience was issued by more than 100 leaders from every continent. That Declaration was an appeal to South Africa to bring its policies into line with the Universal Declaration of Human Rights adopted by the General Assembly of the United Nations.

The Declaration was a good start in mobilising world sentiment to back those in South Africa who acted for equality. The non-whites took heart in learning that they were not alone. And many white supremacists learned for the first time how isolated they were.

Measures of Desperation

Subsequent to the Declaration, the South African Government took the following measures:

- BANNED the African National Congress and the Pan Africanist Congress, the principal protest organisations, and jailed their leaders;
- COERCED the press into strict pro-government censorship and made it almost impossible for new anti-apartheid publications to exist;
- ESTABLISHED an arms industry, more than tripled the military budget, distributed small arms to the white population, enlarged the army, created an extensive white civilian militia;

- ACTIVATED total physical race separation by establishing the first Bantustan in the Transkei—with the aid of emergency police regulations;
- LEGALLY DEFINED protest against apartheid as an act of "sabotage"—an offence ultimately punishable by death;
- PERPETUATED its control through terrorism and violence:
  - Human Rights Day (December 10), 1959—12 South West Africans killed at Windhoek and 40 wounded as they fled police
  - March 21, 1960—72 Africans killed and 186 wounded at Sharpeville by police
  - Before and during the two-year "emergency" in the Transkei—15 Africans killed by police, thousands arrested and imprisoned without trial.

The Choice
The deepening tensions can lead to two alternatives:

Solution [1]
Intensified persecution may lead to violence and armed rebellion once it is clear that peaceful adjustments are no longer possible. As the persecution has been inflicted by one racial group upon all other racial groups, large-scale violence would take the form of a racial war.

This "solution" may be workable. But mass racial extermination will destroy the potential for interracial unity in South Africa and elsewhere.

Therefore, we ask for your *action* to make the following possible.

Solution 2
"Nothing which we have suffered at the hands of the government has turned us from our chosen path of disciplined resistance," said Chief Albert J. Luthuli at Oslo. So there exists another alternative—and the only solution which represents sanity—transition to a society based upon equality for all without regard to colour.

Any solution founded on justice is unattainable until the Government of South Africa is forced by pressures, both internal and external, to come to terms with the demands of the non-white majority. The apartheid republic is a reality today *only because* the peoples and governments of the world have been unwilling to place her in quarantine.

Translate Public Opinion into Public Action

We, therefore, ask all men of goodwill to take action against apartheid in the following manner:

Hold meetings and demonstrations on December 10, Human Rights Day;

Urge your church, union, lodge, or club to observe this day as one of protest;

Urge your Government to support economic sanctions;

Write to your mission to the United Nations urging adoption of a resolution calling for international isolation of South Africa;

Don't buy South Africa's products;

Don't trade or invest in South Africa;

Translate public opinion into public action by explaining facts to all peoples, to groups to which you belong, and to countries of which you are citizens until AN EFFECTIVE INTERNATIONAL QUARANTINE OF APARTHEID IS ESTABLISHED.

"South African Independence"

Speech by Martin Luther King, Jr.

LONDON, ENGLAND, DECEMBER 7, 1964

—◇◇—

I understand that there are South Africans here tonight—some of whom have been involved in the long struggle for freedom there. In our struggle for freedom and justice in the United States, which has also been so long and arduous, we feel a powerful sense of identification with those in the far more deadly struggle for freedom in South Africa. We know how Africans there, and their friends of other races, strove for half a century to win their freedom by non-violent methods. We have honoured Chief Luthuli for his leadership, and we know how this non-violence was only met by increasing violence from the state, increasing repression, culminating in the shootings of Sharpeville and all that has happened since.

Clearly there is much in Mississippi and Alabama to remind South Africans of their own country, yet even in Mississippi we can organise to register Negro voters, we can speak to the press, we can in short organise the people in non-violent action. But in South Africa even the mildest form of non-violent resistance meets with years of imprisonment, and leaders over many years have been restricted and silenced and imprisoned. We can understand how in that situation people felt so desperate that they turned to other methods, such as sabotage.

Today great leaders—Nelson Mandela and Robert Sobukwe— are among many hundreds wasting away in Robben Island prison. Against the massively armed and ruthless state, which uses torture and sadistic forms of interrogation to crush human beings—even driving some to suicide—the militant opposition inside South Africa seems for the moment to be silenced: the mass of the people seems to be contained, seems for the moment unable to break from oppression. I emphasise the word *"seems"* because we can imagine what emotions and plans must be seething below the calm surface of that prosperous police state. We know what emotions are seething in the rest of Africa.

The dangers of a race war—of these dangers we have had repeated and profound warning.

It is in this situation, with the great mass of South Africans denied their humanity, their dignity, denied opportunity, denied all human rights; it is in this situation, with many of the bravest and best South Africans serving long years in prison, with some already executed; in this situation we in America and Britain have a unique responsibility. For it is we, through our investments, through our Governments' failure to act decisively, who are guilty of bolstering up the South African tyranny.

Our responsibility presents us with a unique opportunity. We can join in the one form of non-violent action that could bring freedom and justice to South Africa—the action which African leaders have appealed for—in a massive movement for economic sanctions.

In a world living under the appalling shadow of nuclear weapons do we not recognise the need to perfect the use of economic pressures? Why is trade regarded by all nations and all ideologies as sacred? Why does our Government, and your Government in Britain, refuse to intervene effectively *now,* as if only when there is a bloodbath in South Africa—or a Korea, or a Vietnam—will they recognise the crisis?

If the United Kingdom and the United States decided tomorrow morning not to buy South African goods, not to buy South African gold, to put an embargo on oil; if our investors and capitalists would withdraw their support for that racial tyranny, then apartheid would be brought to an end. Then the majority of South Africans of all races could at last build the shared society they desire.

Though we in the civil rights movement still have a long

and difficult struggle in our own country, increasingly we are recognising our power as voters; already we have made our feelings clear to the President; increasingly we intend to influence American policy in the United Nations and towards South Africa.

"Let My People Go"

South Africa Benefit Speech by
Martin Luther King, Jr.

Hunter College

NEW YORK, NEW YORK, DECEMBER 10, 1965

Africa has been depicted for more than a century as the home of black cannibals and ignorant primitives. Despite volumes of facts contradicting this picture the stereotype persists in books, motion pictures, and other media of communication.

Africa does have spectacular savages and brutes today, but they are not black. They are the sophisticated white rulers of South Africa who profess to be cultured, religious and civilised, but whose conduct and philosophy stamp them unmistakably as modern-day barbarians.

We are in an era in which the issue of human rights is the central question confronting all nations. In this complex struggle an obvious but little-appreciated fact has gained attention—the large majority of the human race is non-white, yet it is that large majority that lives in hideous poverty. While millions enjoy an unexampled opulence in developed nations 10,000 people die of hunger each and every day of the year in the undeveloped world. To assert white supremacy, to invoke white economic and military power to maintain the *status quo* is to foster the danger of international race war. Already the largest nation on earth, Red China, plays seriously with the concept of colour conflict. What does the South African Government contribute to this tense situation? These are the incendiary words of the South African philosophy spoken by its Prime Minister Dr. Verwoerd:

We want to keep South Africa white. Keeping it white can
only mean one thing, namely white domination, not "leadership," not "guidance," but control, supremacy.

The South African Government to make the white supreme has
had to reach into the past and revive the nightmarish ideology
and practices of Nazism. We are witnessing a recrudescence of
that barbarism which murdered more humans than any war in
history. In South Africa today all opposition to white supremacy is condemned as communism, and in its name, due process
is destroyed, a medieval segregation is organised with twentieth
century efficiency and drive, a sophisticated form of slavery is
imposed by a minority upon a majority who are kept in grinding
poverty, the dignity of human personality is defiled and world
opinion is arrogantly defied.

Once more we read of tortures in jails with electric devices,
suicides among prisoners, forced confessions, while in the outside
community ruthless persecution of editors, religious leaders and
political opponents suppresses free speech and a free press.

South Africa says to the world, "We have become a powerful industrial economy, we are too strong to be defeated by paper resolutions of world tribunals, we are immune to protest and
to economic reprisals. We are invulnerable to opposition from
within or without; if our evil offends you, you will have to learn
to live with it."

Increasingly in recent months this conclusion has been echoed
by sober commentators of other countries who disapprove, but
nevertheless assert that there can be no remedy against this for-
midable adversary of human rights.

Do we too acknowledge defeat? Have we tried everything
and failed? In examining this question as Americans we are immediately struck by the fact that the United States moved with
strikingly different energy when it reached a dubious conclusion
that our interests were threatened in the Dominican Republic. We
inundated that small nation with overwhelming force shocking

the world with our zealousness and naked power. With respect to South Africa however, our protest is so muted and peripheral it merely mildly disturbs the sensibilities of the segregationists, while our trade and investments substantially stimulate their economy to greater heights. We pat them on the wrist in permitting racially mixed receptions in our embassy, and by exhibiting films depicting Negro artists. But we give them massive support through American investments in motor and rubber industries, by extending some forty million dollars in loans through our most distinguished banking and financial institutions, by purchasing gold and other minerals mined by black slave labour, by giving them a sugar quota, by maintaining three tracking stations there and by providing them with the prestige of a nuclear reactor built with our technical cooperation and fueled with refined uranium supplied by us.

When it is realised that Great Britain, France and other democratic powers also prop up the economy of South Africa and when to all of this is added the fact that the U.S.S.R. has indicated its willingness to participate in a boycott it is proper to wonder how South Africa can so confidently defy the civilised world. The conclusion is inescapable that it is less sure of its own power, but more sure that the great nations will not sacrifice trade and profit to effectively oppose them. The shame of our nation is that it is objectively an ally of this monstrous government in its grim war with its own black people.

Our default is all the more grievous because one of the blackest pages of our history was our participation in the infamous African slave trade of the 17th century. The rape of Africa was conducted substantially for our benefit to facilitate the growth of our nation and to enhance its commerce. There are few parallels in human history of the period in which Africans were seized and branded like animals, packed into ships' holds like cargo and transported into chattel slavery. Millions suffered agonising death in the middle passage in a holocaust reminiscent of the Nazi slaughter of Jews, Poles and others. We have an obligation of atonement that is not cancelled by the passage of time. Indeed the slave trade in one sense was more understandable than our contemporary policy. There was less sense of humanity in the world three hundred years ago. The slave trade was widely approved by the major powers of the world. The economies of England, Spain and the United States rested heavily on the profits derived from it. Today in our opulent society our reliance on trade with South Africa is infinitesimal in significance. No real national interest impels us to be cautious, gentle, or a good customer of a nation that offends the world's conscience.

Have we the power to be more than peevish with South Africa, but yet refrain from acts of war? To list the extensive economic relations of the great powers with South Africa is to suggest a potent non-violent path. The international potential of non-violence has never been employed. Non-violence has been practised within national borders in India, the United States and in regions of Africa with spectacular success. The time has come fully to utilise non-violence through a massive international boycott which would involve the U.S.S.R., Great Britain, France, the United States, Germany and Japan. Millions of people can personally give expression to their abhorrence of the world's worst racism through such a far flung boycott. No nation professing a concern for man's dignity could avoid assuming its obligations if people of all states and races adopted a firm stand. Nor need we confine an international boycott to South Africa. Rhodesia has earned a place as a target, as has Portugal, colonial master of Angola and Mozambique. The time has come for an international alliance of peoples of all nations against racism.

For the American Negro there is a special relationship with Africa. It is the land of his origin. It was despoiled by invaders, its culture was arrested and concealed to justify white supremacy. The American Negro's ancestors were not only driven into slavery, but their links with their past were severed so that their servitude might be psychological as well as physical. In this period when the American Negro is giving moral leadership and inspiration to his own nation, he must find the resources to aid his suffering brothers in his ancestral homeland. Nor is this aid a one-way street. The civil rights movement in the United States has derived immense inspiration from the successful struggles of those Africans who have attained freedom in their own nations. The fact that black men govern states, are building democratic institutions, sit in world tribunals, and participate in global decision-making gives every Negro a needed sense of dignity.

In this effort the American Negro will not be alone. As this meeting testifies there are many white people who know that liberty is indivisible. Even more inspiring is the fact that in South Africa itself incredibly brave white people are risking their careers, their homes and their lives in the cause of human justice. Nor is this a plea to Negroes to fight on two fronts. The struggle for freedom forms one long front crossing oceans and mountains. The brotherhood of man is not confined within a narrow, limited circle of select people. It is felt everywhere in the world, it is an international sentiment of surpassing strength and because this is true when men of good will finally unite they will be invincible.

Through recent anthropological discoveries science has substantially established that the cradle of humanity is Africa. The earliest creatures who passed the divide between animal and man seem to have first emerged in East and South Africa. Professor Raymond Dart described this historical epoch as the moment when man "trembled on the brink of humanity." A million years later in the same place some men of South Africa are again "trembling on the brink of humanity," but instead of advancing from pre-human to human they are reversing the process and are travelling backward in time from human to pre-human.

Civilization has come a long way, it has far still to go and it cannot afford to be set back by resolute wicked men. Negroes were dispersed over thousands of miles and over many continents yet today they have found each other again. Negro and white have been separated for centuries by evil men and evil myths. But they have found each other. The powerful unity of Negro with Negro and white with Negro is stronger than the most potent and entrenched racism. The whole human race will benefit when it ends the abomination that has diminished the stature of man for too long. This is the task to which we are called by the suffering in South Africa and our response should be swift and unstinting. Out of this struggle will come the glorious reality of the family of man.

"Invitation to South Africa"

Letter from Martin Luther King, Jr.,
to the South African Embassy

FEBRUARY 9, 1966

South African Embassy
Suite 1616
225 Baronne Street
New Orleans, Louisiana

Dear Sir:

I have been invited to lecture in South Africa by two outstanding student groups of your country. The National Union of South African Students has invited me to address its 1966 Congress in July and the Students' Visiting Lecturers Organisation of the University of Cape Town invited me to deliver the T.B. Davie Memorial Lecture. I have accepted both of these invitations and I have a great interest in visiting South Africa in order to exchange cultural and human rights and concern. My visit would be purely as a lecturer.

My schedule here in the United States would not allow me to stay over the period involved in the lectures and one or two receptions that have been requested by the students. I would also be interested in spending a few hours talking with some of the religious leaders.

In the light of this, I am herewith applying for a visa to South Africa in order to make a personal appearance for these engagements. I would appreciate all of the cooperation that you can give.

Very sincerely yours,
Martin Luther King, Jr.

"On the World Taking a Stand on Rhodesia"

Comment by Martin Luther King, Jr.

PARIS, FRANCE, OCTOBER 25, 1965

MLK: I think that it is very urgent for the world, for all of the nations of the world to take a stand against this attempt on the part of the Government of Rhodesia to turn the clock of history back. Rhodesia, Southern Rhodesia will become another South Africa and the world cannot stand another South Africa. Another one only augments the problem and I think it is very urgent that a positive stand be taken against Southern Rhodesia and that they not be allowed to engage in this kind of dastardly act, blocking representation on the part of the African people themselves.

Q: *What do you think should be done?*

MLK: I think the UN should be the force that will stand behind the British government in not granting independence to S. Rhodesia as it is presently seeking it. I'm all for independence but it must be an independence with a one-man, one-vote idea behind it. And I think the British Government should stand firm and not grant this independence, and I think the UN should stand behind Britain.

"Racism and the World House"

Statement by Martin Luther King, Jr.

From *Where Do We Go from Here:
Chaos or Community?*

1967

———⬥———

Among the moral imperatives of our time, we are challenged to work all over the world with unshakable determination to wipe out the last vestiges of racism. As early as 1906 W. E. B. Du Bois prophesied that "the problem of the twentieth century will be the problem of the color line." Now as we stand two-thirds into this exciting period of history we know full well that racism is still that hound of hell which dogs the tracks of our civilization.

Racism is no mere American phenomenon. Its vicious grasp knows no geographical boundaries. In fact, racism and its perennial ally—economic exploitation—provide the key to understanding most of the international complications of this generation.

The classic example of organized and institutionalized racism is the Union of South Africa. Its national policy and practice are the incarnation of the doctrine of white supremacy in the midst of a population which is overwhelmingly black. But the tragedy of South Africa is not simply in its own policy; it is the fact that the racist government of South Africa is virtually made possible by the economic policies of the United States and Great Britain, two countries which profess to be the moral bastions of our Western world.

In country after country we see white men building empires on the sweat and suffering of colored people. Portugal continues its practices of slave labor and subjugation in Angola; the Ian Smith government in Rhodesia continues to enjoy the support of British-based industry and private capital, despite the stated opposition of British government policy. Even in the case of the little country of South West Africa we find the powerful nations of the world incapable of taking a moral position against South Africa, though the smaller country is under the trusteeship of the United Nations. Its policies are controlled by South Africa and its manpower is lured into the mines under slave-labor conditions.

During the Kennedy administration there was some awareness of the problems that breed in the racist and exploitative conditions throughout the colored world, and a temporary concern emerged to free the United States from its complicity though the effort was only on a diplomatic level. Through our ambassador to the United Nations, Adlai Stevenson, there emerged the beginnings of an intelligent approach to the colored peoples of the world. However, there remained little or no attempt to deal with the economic aspects of racist exploitation. We have been notoriously silent about the more than $700 million of American capital which props up the system of apartheid, not to mention the billions of dollars in trade and the military alliances which are maintained under the pretext of fighting Communism in Africa.

Nothing provides the Communists with a better climate for expansion and infiltration than the continued alliance of our nation with racism and exploitation throughout the world. And if we are not diligent in our determination to root out the last vestiges of racism in our dealings with the rest of the world, we may soon see the sins of our fathers visited upon ours and succeeding generations. For the conditions which are so classically represented in Africa are present also in Asia and in our own back yard in Latin America.

Everywhere in Latin America one finds a tremendous resentment of the United States, and that resentment is always strongest among the poorer and darker peoples of the continent. The life and destiny of Latin America are in the hands of United States corporations. The decisions affecting the lives of South Americans are ostensibly made by their government, but there are almost no legitimate democracies alive in the whole continent. The other governments are dominated by huge and exploitative cartels that rob Latin America of her resources while turning over a small rebate to a few members of a corrupt aristocracy, which in turn invests not in its own country for its own people's welfare but in the banks of Switzerland and the playgrounds of the world.

Here we see racism in its more sophisticated form: neo-colonialism. The Bible and the annals of history are replete with tragic stories of one brother robbing another of his birthright and thereby insuring generations of strife and enmity. We can hardly escape such a judgment in Latin America, any more than we have been able to escape the harvest of hate sown in Vietnam by a century of French exploitation.

There is the convenient temptation to attribute the current turmoil and bitterness throughout the world to the presence of a Communist conspiracy to undermine Europe and America, but the potential explosiveness of our world situation is much more attributable to disillusionment with the promises of Christianity and technology.

The revolutionary leaders of Africa, Asia and Latin America have virtually all received their education in the capitals of the West. Their earliest training often occurred in Christian missionary schools. Here their sense of dignity was established and they learned that all men were sons of God. In recent years their countries have been invaded by automobiles, Coca-Cola and Hollywood, so that even remote villages have become aware of the wonders and blessings available to God's white children.

Once the aspirations and appetites of the world have been whetted by the marvels of Western technology and the self image of a people awakened by religion, one cannot hope to keep people locked out of the earthly kingdom of wealth, health and happiness. Either they share in the blessings of the world or they organize to break down and overthrow those structures or governments which stand in the way of their goals.

Former generations could not conceive of such luxury, but their children now take this vision and demand that it become a reality. And when they look around and see that the only people who do not share in the abundance of Western technology are colored people, it is an almost inescapable conclusion that their condition and their exploitation are somehow related to their color and the racism of the white Western world.

This is a treacherous foundation for a world house. Racism can well be that corrosive evil that will bring down the curtain on Western civilization. Arnold Toynbee has said that some twenty-six civilizations have risen upon the face of the earth. Almost all of them have descended into the junk heaps of destruction. The decline and fall of these civilizations, according to Toynbee, was not caused by external invasions but by internal decay. They failed to respond creatively to the challenges impinging upon them. If Western civilization does not now respond constructively to the challenge to banish racism, some future historian will have to say that a great civilization died because it lacked the soul and commitment to make justice a reality for all men.

PART III

Breaking the Chains of Colonialism: The Rise of Peoples of Color in the Third World

An evil system got started in the world known as colonialism. And the great nations of Europe moved into Asia and Africa, exploiting the people economically, dominating them politically. It came to the point that the vast majority of the people of Asia and Africa were dominated by some foreign power. . . . Most of these people were . . . trampled over by quarreling powers. People fought for independence.

> — "Discerning the Signs of History," a sermon delivered at Ebenezer Baptist Church, Atlanta, Georgia, November 15, 1964

Introduction

D r. King brought a keen sensitivity to the history of colonialism and its subversive influence on people of color throughout the globe. He understood and occasionally referred to the tragic series of events that led European nation-states to establish colonies on other continents, and particularly Africa and Asia, in the period from the fifteenth to the twentieth centuries. Colonialism for King involved not only territorial expansion but also the domination and subjugation of people of color by Europeans, and he saw a strong ideological link between this practice and the evils of racism and imperialism. King was also mindful of how colonialism encouraged forms of internal oppression among the colonized, especially in cases where political leaders and government officials in the colonies abused and exploited their subjects for personal gain.

Eight documents make up part III of *"In a Single Garment of Destiny."* The focus is on the political and economic control of Africans and Asians by Europeans, with attention, in some of the documents, to the shared experiences and obligations between black Americans and people of color elsewhere in the world. Most of King's reflections on colonialism also highlighted the struggles of Africans and Asians against white supremacist values and structures, and he frequently addressed the need for people of color to realize their common struggles while relying primarily on themselves in vital areas of life in order to effect their own liberation, despite the openness to support from whites. The four statements, two sermons, and two articles reveal King's belief that black Americans and other people of color should work together in attacking colonialism, racism, and imperialism as perennial allies.

King's statement "Invitation to Ghana," put out in March 1957, a month before he attended the independence celebration in that nation, is the first document in part III. In it, King mentioned the new courage, self-respect, dignity, and inspiration that his people in America experienced as a result of Ghana's independence from British colonial domination, and he noted how this historic event highlighted the fact that "elementary rights of citizenship and equality" were still unrealized for millions of people of color. King's statement must be considered in conjunction with his sermon "The Birth of a New Nation," preached at the Dexter Avenue Baptist Church in Montgomery, Alabama, on April 7, 1957, shortly after his return from Ghana. In this sermon, King drew upon the biblical account of Exodus to explain Ghana's crusade against colonialism, declaring that the Exodus story—the flight of the Hebrew people from Egyptian bondage to the Promised Land—is really the story of every people groping for freedom under the political and economic rule of foreign powers. Apparently, King thought that his people in America had much to learn from Ghana about the cost of freedom.

King's statement "Introduction to Southwest Africa: The U.N.'s Stepchild" is really his personal impression of Africa's move beyond colonialism toward freedom and independence. This statement is included in part III because it fits well into the larger corpus of King's documents on the relationship between European colonialism and racism. Here King expressed a particular concern for Southwest Africa, which struggled under the sovereignty of South Africa. Evidently, King felt that the United Nations had a special role in eliminating this problem, as did the representatives of world Christianity. He delighted in the fact that Michael Scott, an Anglican priest who had worked with unwanted lepers in South Africa, was exemplifying the potential power of the Christian faith by speaking out on behalf of the Herero people of Southwest Africa. For King, European colonial practices, much like racism and imperialism, blatantly contradicted both the Christian ethic and the democratic claims of Western society.

"My Talk with Ben Bella" appeared in the *New York Amsterdam News* on October 27, 1962. It covers King's conversation with Premier Ben Bella of the New Algerian Republic, and it is included here not only because it reinforces the idea that black

Americans and Africans are related and engaged in a common struggle but also because it captures the meeting of the minds of two of the most powerful figures in the black world at that time. Apparently, both King and Bella were deeply concerned about the international implications of colonialism and racial segregation. As suggested earlier, one of the most striking features of the global King was his conversations and collaborative efforts with other world leaders around the need to not only challenge the legitimacy of colonialism and its racist implications but also its capitalistic and militaristic undertones.

In King's statement "The Negro Looks at Africa," dated December 8, 1962, King reiterated concerns expressed in many of his other statements on Africa, but he was particularly interested in black America's relationship to "the new independent nations of Africa" and in how this was instilling in the so-called Negro a "growing awareness of his world citizenship." King notes that "colonialism and segregation are nearly synonymous," particularly in their tendencies toward economic exploitation, political domination, and the degradation of human personality. King also raised the need for "Negro Americans" to develop a deeper interest in U.S. policy toward Africa and for "a broader use" of their participation in the diplomatic corps that served "the independent and emergent nations" of Africa. This viewpoint was consistent with King's belief that black Americans should assume a vanguard role in the crusade against both colonialism and racism. King maintained, as in his *Where Do We Go from Here: Chaos or Community?* (1967), that the hope of Africans and Asians struggling under the yoke of colonialism rested largely with "the American Negro" and his success in reforming the structures of racist imperialism from within, thereby turning the technology and wealth of the West toward the goal of freeing the world from want.

Although three documents in part III focus on India's struggle for independence, they provide a significant angle from which to assess King's attitude toward all Asians who resisted European colonizers and their racist and imperialistic ventures. King spoke to the deep ties between black Americans and the people of Asia, and he saw certain shared values that moved across the cultural boundaries that separated his people in America from both Asians and Africans. In King's "Palm Sunday Sermon on Mohandas K. Gandhi," important references are made to Gandhi and his success in mobilizing Indians in their nonviolent assault on British colonial domination, an effort that led to independence in 1947. Gandhi is also treated as a saintly figure who sought to free the people of India from a vicious caste system that was encouraged by a colonialist ethic—and that threatened them from within. The fact that King devoted a sermon to the memory of Gandhi and India's anticolonial crusade on Palm Sunday 1959 is telling enough, for it highlighted his ability to frame his arguments against colonialism in religious and ethical terms.

In "My Trip to the Land of Gandhi," published in *Ebony* in July 1959, King turned to the question of what he had learned from Gandhi and the Indian people's independence struggle. Between February 2 and March 10, 1959, King toured India and met and talked with some of Gandhi's relatives and with Prime Minister Jawaharlal Nehru, an admirer of Gandhi. By his own admission, King left India with a greater appreciation of its people and their anticolonial cause, and with a deeper conviction that nonviolent resistance is "the most potent weapon available to oppressed people" in their effort to win genuine freedom. "My Trip to the Land of Gandhi" is provided here because it reveals King's growing and maturing perspective on how racism, colonialism, and imperialism might best be removed from the face of the earth. As noted earlier, King's travels to various parts of the world figured prominently in this kind of growth and maturation process.

The final document in part III is King's article on Jawaharlal Nehru, written as a tribute to the Indian leader after his death. Prepared for the Nehru centenary volume, *Legacy of Nehru* (1965), at the request of editor K. Natwar-Singh, the article examines the significance of Nehru for the crusade against colonialism, racism, and imperialism. King submitted the article on February 8, 1965, almost two months after the December 15, 1964, deadline. In any case, the unpublished version is included because it says as much about King's attitude toward colonialism and imperialism as it does about his perception of Nehru and his place in Indian and world history.

The systems of colonialism that King critiqued and hoped to eradicate no longer exist, and we now live in what some writers call the age of postcolonialism. But much is still said and written about the tragic economic, political, and cultural legacy of European colonialism, and, in the context of this discussion, King's ideas still hold some relevance. This is especially true when one considers the developing trends in neocolonialism over the last two generations, developments that have made it possible for the former colonizers to benefit disproportionately from the economic arrangements they created with their former colonies. In other words, the so-called developed countries of the world still dominate and exploit the so-called undeveloped and underdeveloped nations through the networks of global capitalism. King saw this practice emerging in the last years of his life, as he surveyed the long, ambivalent, complex, and often volatile relationship between white and dark-skinned peoples, and he referred to neocolonialism as an arrangement that no reputable country could accept.

The economic domination and exploitation of poor nations by rich countries is antithetical to King's vision of a "world house," or a truly global beloved community, and this must cease to be the prevailing order of contemporary global interaction. The healing and wholeness that King recommended for our world will not come through U.S. and European dominance in world affairs but through international relationships that are driven by a commitment to human rights, genuine economic prosperity and equality, and the flowering of democratic freedoms. Indeed, King's legacy of thought and praxis, as the documents in part III of this volume indicate, is an innovative challenge to the colonial and neocolonial mindset, and to the traditional ways of thinking about how nations should relate to each other.

"Invitation to Ghana"

Statement by Martin Luther King, Jr.

MONTGOMERY, ALABAMA, MARCH 1957

—◇◇◇—

When I received from Prime Minister Nkrumah the invitation to the Independence Ceremonies in Ghana, I felt that I held in my hand a fraternal greeting to the Negro people of Montgomery whose tenacious struggle and sacrifices had won the admiration of all freedom-loving people. There is necessarily a close bond between the American Negro and the Negroes of the Gold Coast, since a very large number of us trace our ancestry to that part of Africa which is now Ghana.

The achievement of a free and independent Negro Nation in Africa highlights the fact that in our nation elementary rights of citizenship and equality are still unrealized for millions, and in particular, for the Southern Negro. This condition explains the intense interest and pride we have in this historic event.

Ghana represents a victorious sector in the world-wide movement of colonial peoples toward the dawn of freedom. Our own struggle in the United States is a part of this great democratic upsurge, and the knowledge that Ghana has won liberation inspires us with the confidence that our fight for justice will be won not in a distant tomorrow, but in a day closer at hand than we have heretofore realized.

"The Birth of a New Nation"

Sermon by Martin Luther King, Jr.

Dexter Avenue Baptist Church

MONTGOMERY, ALABAMA, APRIL 7, 1957

—◇◆◇—

I want to preach this morning from the subject: "The Birth of a New Nation." And I would like to use as a basis for our thinking together, a story that has long since been stenciled on the mental sheets of succeeding generations. It is the story of the Exodus, the story of the flight of the Hebrew people from the bondage of Egypt, through the wilderness, and finally to the Promised Land. It's a beautiful story. I had the privilege the other night of seeing the story in movie terms in New York City, entitled *The Ten Commandments*, and I came to see it in all of its beauty—the struggle of Moses, the struggle of his devoted followers as they sought to get out of Egypt. And they finally moved onto the wilderness and toward the Promised Land. This is something of the story of every people struggling for freedom. It is the first story of man's explicit quest for freedom. And it demonstrates the stages that seem to inevitably follow the quest for freedom.

Prior to March the sixth, 1957, there existed a country known as the Gold Coast. This country was a colony of the British Empire. This country was situated in that vast continent known as Africa. I'm sure you know a great deal about Africa, that continent with some two hundred million people, and it extends and covers a great deal of territory. There are many familiar names associated with Africa that you would probably remember, and there are some countries in Africa that many people never realize. For instance, Egypt is in Africa. And there is that vast area of North Africa with Egypt and Ethiopia, with Tunisia and Algeria and Morocco and Libya. Then you might move to South Africa and you think of that extensive territory known as the Union

58

of South Africa. There is that capital city Johannesburg that you read so much about these days. Then there is central Africa with places like Rhodesia and the Belgian Congo and then there is East Africa with places like Kenya and Tanganyika, and places like Uganda and other very powerful countries right there. And then you move over to West Africa, where you find the French West Africa and Nigeria, and Liberia and Sierra Leone and places like that. And it is in this spot, in this section of Africa, that we find the Gold Coast, there in West Africa.

You also know that for years and for centuries, Africa has been one of the most exploited continents in the history of the world. It's been the "Dark Continent." It's been the continent that has suffered all of the pain and the affliction that could be mustered up by other nations and it is that continent which has experienced slavery, which has experienced all of the lowest standards that we can think about, and it's been brought into being by the exploitation inflicted upon it by other nations.

And this country, the Gold Coast, was a part of this extensive continent known as Africa. It's a little country there in West Africa about ninety-one thousand miles in area, with a population of about five million people, a little more than four and a half million. And it stands there with its capital city Accra. For years the Gold Coast was exploited and dominated and trampled over. The first European settlers came in there about 1444, the Portuguese, and they started legitimate trade with the people in the Gold Coast. They started dealing with them with their gold, and in turn they gave them guns and ammunition and gunpowder and that type of thing. Well, pretty soon America was discovered a few years later in the fourteen hundreds, and then the British West Indies. And all of these growing discoveries brought about the slave trade.

You remember it started in America in 1619. And there was a big scramble for power in Africa. With the growth of the slave trade, there came into Africa, into the Gold Coast in particular, not only the Portuguese but also the Swedes and the Danes and the Dutch and the British. And all of these nations competed with each other to win the power of the Gold Coast so that they could exploit these people for commercial reasons and sell them into slavery.

Finally, in 1850, Britain won out, and she gained possession of the total territorial expansion of the Gold Coast. From 1850 to 1957, March sixth, the Gold Coast was a colony of the British Empire. And as a colony she suffered all of the injustices, all of the exploitation, all of the humiliation that comes as a result of colonialism. But like all slavery, like all domination, like all exploitation, it came to the point that the people got tired of it.

And that seems to be the long story of history. There seems to be a throbbing desire, there seems to be an internal desire for freedom within the soul of every man. And it's there: it might not break forth in the beginning, but eventually it breaks out. Men realize that, that freedom is something basic. To rob a man of his freedom is to take from him the essential basis of his manhood. To take from him his freedom is to rob him of something of God's image. To paraphrase the words of Shakespeare's *Othello*: "Who steals my purse steals trash; 'tis, something, nothing; 'twas mine, 'tis his, has been the slave of thousands. But he who filches from me my freedom robs me of that which not enriches him, but makes me poor indeed."

There is something in the soul that cries out for freedom. There is something deep down within the very soul of man that reaches out for Canaan. Men cannot be satisfied with Egypt. They try to adjust to it for a while. Many men have vested interests in Egypt, and they are slow to leave. Egypt makes it profitable to them, some people profit by Egypt. The vast majority, the masses of people never profit by Egypt, and they are never content with it. And eventually they rise up and begin to cry out for Canaan's land.

And so these people got tired. It had a long history. As far back as 1844, the chiefs themselves of the Gold Coast rose up and came together and revolted against the British Empire and the other powers that were in existence at that time dominating the Gold Coast. They revolted, saying that they wanted to govern themselves. But these powers clamped down on them, and the British said that we will not let you go.

About 1909, a young man was born on the twelfth of September. History didn't know at that time what that young man had in his mind. His mother and father, illiterate, not a part of the powerful tribal life of Africa, not chiefs at all, but humble people. And that boy grew up, he went to school, at Achimota for a while in Africa, and then he finished there with honors and decided to work his way to America. And he landed to America one day with about fifty dollars in his pocket in terms of pounds, getting ready to get an education. And he went down to Pennsylvania, to Lincoln University. He started studying there, and he started reading the great insights of the philosophers, he started reading the great insights of the ages. And he finished there and took his theological degree there and preached awhile around Philadelphia and other areas as he was in the country. And went over to the University of Pennsylvania and took up a master's there in philosophy and sociology. All the years that he stood in America, he was poor, he had to work hard. He says in his autobiography how he worked as a bellhop in hotels, as a dishwasher, and during the summer how he worked as a waiter trying to struggle through school. [*recording interrupted*] . . .

"I want to go back to West Africa, the land of my people, my native land. There is some work to be done there." He got a ship and went to London and stopped for a while by London School of Economy and picked up another degree there. Then while in London, he came, he started thinking about Pan-Africanism, and the problem of how to free his people from colonialism. For as he said, he always realized that colonialism was made for domination and for exploitation. It was made to keep a certain group down and exploit that group economically for the advantage of another. He studied and thought about all of this, and one day he decided to go back to Africa.

He got to Africa and he was immediately elected the executive secretary of the United Party of the Gold Coast. And he worked hard and he started getting a following. And the people in this party, the old, the people who had had their hands on the plow for a long time, thought he was pushing a little too fast, and they got a little jealous of his influence. And so finally he had to break from the United Party of the Gold Coast, and in 1949 he organized the Convention People's Party. It was this party that started out working for the independence of the Gold Coast. He started out in a humble way, urging his people to unite for freedom. And urging the officials of the British Empire to give them freedom. They were slow to respond, but the masses of people were with him, and they had united to become the most powerful and influential party that had ever been organized in that section of Africa.

He started writing, and his companions with him and many of them started writing so much that the officials got afraid, and they put them in jail, and Nkrumah himself was finally placed in jail for several years because he was a seditious man. He was an agitator. He was imprisoned on the basis of sedition. And he was placed there to stay in prison for many years, but he had inspired some people outside of prison. They got together just a few months after he'd been in prison and elected him the prime minister while he was in prison. For a while the British officials tried to keep him there, and Gbedemah said—one of his close associates, the minister of finance, Mr. Gbedemah—said that that night the people were getting ready to go down to the jail and get him out, but Gbedemah said, "This isn't the way, we can't do it like this, violence will break out and we will defeat our purpose." But the British Empire saw that they had better let him out. And in a few hours Kwame Nkrumah was out of jail, the prime minister of the Gold Coast. He was placed there for fifteen years but he only served eight or nine months. And now he comes out, the prime minister of the Gold Coast.

And this was the struggling that had been going on for years. It was now coming to the point that this little nation was moving toward its independence. Then came the continual agitation, the continual resistance, so that the British Empire saw that it could no longer rule the Gold Coast. And they agreed that on the sixth of March, 1957, they would release this nation, that this nation would no longer be a colony of the British Empire, that this nation would be a sovereign nation within the British Commonwealth. All of this was because of the persistent protest, the continual agitation on the part of Prime Minister Kwame Nkrumah and the other leaders who worked along with him and the masses of people who were willing to follow.

So that day finally came. It was a great day. The week ahead was a great week. They had been preparing for this day for many years, and now it was here. People coming in from all over the world. They had started getting in by the second of March. Seventy nations represented to come to say to this new nation: "We greet you. And we give you our moral support. We hope for you God's guidance as you move now into the realm of independence." From America, itself, more than a hundred persons: the press, the diplomatic guests, and the prime ministers' guests. And oh, it was a beautiful experience to see some of the leading persons on the scene of civil rights in America on hand to say, "Greetings to you," as this new nation was born. Look over, to my right is Adam Powell, to my left is Charles Diggs, to my right again is Ralph Bunche. To the other side is Her Majesty's first minister of Jamaica, Manning, Ambassador [Richard L.] Jones of Liberia. All of these people from America, Mordecai Johnson, Horace Mann Bond, all of these people just going over to say, "We want to greet you and we want you to know that you have our moral support as you grow." Then you look out and see the vice president of the United States, you see A. Philip Randolph, you see all of the people who have stood in the forefront of the struggle for civil rights over the years, coming over to Africa to say we bid you Godspeed. This was a great day not only for Nkrumah, but for the whole of the Gold Coast. There, then came Tuesday, March the fifth, many events leading up to it. That night, we walked into the closing of Parliament. The closing of the old Parliament. The old Parliament, which was, which presided over by the British Empire. The old Parliament which designated colonialism and imperialism. Now that Parliament is closing. That was a great sight and a great picture and a great scene. We sat there that night, just about five hundred able to get in there. People, thousands and thousands of people waiting outside, just about five hundred in there, and we were fortunate enough to be sitting there at that moment as guests of the prime minister. At that hour we noticed Prime Minister Nkrumah walking in, with all of his ministers, with his justices of the Supreme Court of the Gold Coast, and with all of the people of the Convention People's Party, the leaders of that party. Nkrumah came up to make his closing speech to the old Gold Coast. There was something old now passing away.

The thing that impressed me more than anything else that night was the fact that when Nkrumah walked in, and his other ministers who had been in prison with him, they didn't come in with the crowns and all of the garments of kings, but they walked in with prison caps and the coats that they had lived with for all of the months that they had been in prison. Nkrumah stood up and made his closing speech to Parliament with the little cap that he wore in prison for several months and the coat that he wore in prison for several months, and all of his ministers round about him. That was a great hour. An old Parliament passing away. And then at twelve o'clock that night we walked out. As we walked out, we noticed all over the polo grounds almost a half a million people. They had waited for this hour and this moment for years.

As we walked out of the door and looked at that beautiful building, we looked up to the top of it. And there was a little flag that had been flowing around the sky for many years. It was the Union Jack flag of the Gold Coast, the British flag, you see. But at twelve o'clock that night we saw a little flag coming down and another flag went up. The old Union Jack flag came down and the new flag of Ghana went up. This was a new nation now, a new nation being born. And when Prime Minister Nkrumah stood up before his people out in the polo ground and said, "We are no longer a British colony, we are a free, sovereign people," all over that vast throng of people we could see tears. And I stood there thinking about so many things. Before I knew it, I started weeping. I was crying for joy. And I knew about all of the struggles, and all of the pain, and all of the agony that these people had gone through for this moment.

After Nkrumah had made that final speech, it was about twelve-thirty now. And we walked away. And we could hear little children six years old and old people eighty and ninety years old walking the streets of Accra crying: "Freedom! Freedom!" They couldn't say it in the sense that we'd say it, many of them don't speak English too well, but they had their accents and it could ring out "free-doom!" They were crying it in a sense that they had never heard it before. And I could hear that old Negro spiritual once more crying out: "Free at last, free at last, Great God Almighty, I'm free at last." They were experiencing that in their very souls. And everywhere we turned, we could hear it ringing out from the housetops. We could hear it from every corner, every nook and crook of the community: "Freedom! Freedom!" This was the birth of a new nation. This was the breaking aloose from Egypt.

Wednesday morning the official opening of Parliament was held. There again we were able to get on the inside. There Nkrumah made his new speech. And now the prime minister of the Gold Coast with no superior, with all of the power that [Harold] Macmillan of England has, with all of the power that [Jawaharlal] Nehru of India has, now a free nation, now the prime minister of a sovereign nation. Duchess of Kent walked in, the duchess of Kent who represented the queen of England, no longer had authority now. She was just a passing visitor now. The night before she was the official leader and spokesman for the queen, thereby the power behind the throne of the Gold Coast. But now it's Ghana, it's a new nation now, and she's just an official visitor like M. L. King and Ralph Bunche, and Coretta King and everybody else, because this is a new nation. A new Ghana has come into being. And now Nkrumah stands the leader of that great nation, and when he drives out, the people standing around the streets of the city after Parliament is open, cry out: "All hail, Nkrumah!" The name of Nkrumah crowning around the whole city, everybody crying this name because they knew he had suffered for them, he had sacrificed for them, he'd gone to jail for them. This was the birth of a new nation.

This nation was now out of Egypt and had crossed the Red Sea. Now it will confront its wilderness. Like any breaking aloose from Egypt, there is a wilderness ahead. There is a problem of adjustment. Nkrumah realizes that. There is always this wilderness standing before him. For instance, it's a one crop country, cocoa mainly. Sixty percent of the cocoa of the world comes from the Gold Coast or from Ghana. In order to make the economic system more stable, it will be necessary to industrialize. Cocoa is too fluctuating to base a whole economy on that. So there is the necessity of industrializing. Nkrumah said to me that one of the first things that he will do is to work toward industrialization.

And also he plans to work toward the whole problem of increasing the cultural standards of the community. Still ninety percent of the people are illiterate, and it is necessary to lift the whole standard of the community in order to make it possible to stand up in the free world. Yes, there is a wilderness ahead, though it is my hope that even people from America will go to Africa as immigrants, right there to the Gold Coast and lend their technical assistance. For there is great need and rich, there are rich opportunities there. Right now is the time that American Negroes can lend their technical assistance to a growing new nation. I was very happy to see already, people who have moved in and making good. The son of the late president of Bennett College, Dr. Jones, is there, who started an insurance company and making good, going to the top. A doctor from Brooklyn, New York, had just come in that week and his wife is also a dentist, and they are living there now, going in there and working and the people love them. There will be hundreds and thousands of people, I'm sure, going over to make for the growth of this new nation. And Nkrumah made it very clear to me that he would welcome any persons coming there as immigrants and to live there. Now don't think that because they have five million people the nation can't grow, that that's a small nation to be overlooked. Never forget the fact that when America was born in 1776, when it received its independence from the British Empire, there were fewer, less than four million people in America, and today it's more than a hundred and sixty million. So never underestimate a people because it's small now. America was smaller than Ghana when it was born.

There is a great day ahead. The future is on its side. It's going now through the wilderness. But the Promised Land is ahead.

And I want to take just a few more minutes as I close to say three or four things that this reminds us of and things that it says. Things that we must never forget as we ourselves find ourselves breaking aloose from an evil Egypt, trying to move through the wilderness toward the promised land of cultural integration: Ghana has something to say to us. It says to us first, the oppressor never voluntarily gives freedom to the oppressed. You have to work for it. And if Nkrumah and the people of the Gold Coast had not stood up persistently, revolting against the system, it would still be a colony of the British Empire. Freedom is never given to anybody. For the oppressor has you in domination because he plans to keep you there, and he never voluntarily gives it up. And that is where the strong resistance comes. Privileged classes never give up their privileges without strong resistance.

So don't go out this morning with any illusions. Don't go back into your homes and around Montgomery thinking that the Montgomery City Commission and that all of the forces in the leadership of the South will eventually work out this thing for Negroes, it's going to work out, it's going to roll in on the wheels of inevitability. If we wait for it to work itself out, it will *never* be worked out! Freedom only comes through persistent revolt, through persistent agitation, through persistently rising up against the system of evil. The bus protest is just the beginning. Buses are integrated in Montgomery, but that is just the beginning. And don't sit down and do nothing now because the buses are integrated, because, if you stop now, we will be in the dungeons of segregation and discrimination for another hundred years. And our children and our children's children will suffer all of the bondage that we have lived under for years. It never comes voluntarily. We've got to keep on keeping on in order to gain freedom. It never comes like that. It would be fortunate if the people in power had sense enough to go on and give up, but they don't do it like that. It is not done voluntarily, but it is done through the pressure that comes about from people who are oppressed.

If there had not been a Gandhi in India with all of his noble followers, India would have never been free. If there had not been an Nkrumah and his followers in Ghana, Ghana would still be a British colony. If there had not been abolitionists in America, both Negro and white, we might still stand today in the dungeons of slavery. And then because there have been, in every period, there are always those people in every period of human history who don't mind getting their necks cut off, who don't mind being persecuted and discriminated and kicked about, because they know that freedom is never given out, but it comes through the persistent and the continual agitation and revolt on the part of those who are caught in the system. Ghana teaches us that.

It says to us another thing. It reminds us of the fact that a nation or a people can break aloose from oppression without violence. Nkrumah says in the first two pages of his autobiography, which was published on the sixth of March—a great book which you ought to read—he said that he had studied the social systems of social philosophers and he started studying the life of Gandhi and his techniques. And he said that in the beginning he could not see how they could ever get aloose from colonialism without armed revolt, without armies and ammunition, rising up. Then he says after he continued to study Gandhi and continued to study this technique, he came to see that the only way was through nonviolent positive action. And he called his program "positive action." And it's a beautiful thing, isn't it? That here is a nation that is now free, and it is free without rising up with arms and with ammunition. It is free through nonviolent means. Because of that the British Empire will not have the bitterness for Ghana that she has for China, so to speak. Because of that when the British Empire leaves Ghana, she leaves with a different attitude than she would have left with if she had been driven out by armies. We've got to revolt in such a way that after revolt is over we can live with people as their brothers and their sisters. Our aim must never be to defeat them or humiliate them.

On the night of the State Ball, standing up talking with some people, Mordecai Johnson called my attention to the fact that Prime Minister Kwame Nkrumah was there dancing with the duchess of Kent. And I said, "Isn't this something? Here is the once-serf, the once-slave, now dancing with the lord on an equal plane." And that is done because there is no bitterness. These two nations will be able to live together and work together because the breaking aloose was through nonviolence and not through violence.

The aftermath of nonviolence is the creation of the beloved community. The aftermath of nonviolence is redemption. The aftermath of nonviolence is reconciliation. The aftermath of violence are emptiness and bitterness. This is the thing I'm concerned about. Let us fight passionately and unrelentingly for the goals of justice and peace. But let's be sure that our hands are clean in this struggle. Let us never fight with falsehood and violence and hate and malice, but always fight with love, so that, when the day comes that the walls of segregation have completely crumbled in Montgomery, that we will be able to live with people as their brothers and sisters. Oh, my friends, our aim must be not to defeat Mr. Engelhardt, not to defeat Mr. Sellers and Mr. Gayle and Mr. Parks. Our aim must be to defeat the evil that's in them. But our aim must be to win the friendship of Mr. Gayle, and Mr. Sellers and Mr. Engelhardt. We must come to the point of seeing that our ultimate aim is to live with all men as brothers and sisters under God, and not be their enemies or anything that goes with that type of relationship. And this is one thing that Ghana teaches us: that you can break aloose from evil through nonviolence, through a lack of bitterness. Nkrumah says in his book: "When I came out of prison, I was not bitter toward Britain. I came out merely with the determination to free my people from the colonialism and imperialism that had been inflicted upon them by the British. But

I came out with no bitterness." And because of that, this world will be a better place in which to live.

There's another thing that Ghana reminds us. I'm coming to the conclusion now. Ghana reminds us that freedom never comes on a silver platter. It's never easy. Ghana reminds us that whenever you break out of Egypt, you better get ready for stiff backs. You better get ready for some homes to be bombed. You better get ready for some churches to be bombed. You better get ready for a lot of nasty things to be said about you, because you getting out of Egypt. And whenever you break aloose from Egypt, the initial response of the Egyptian is bitterness. It never comes with ease. It comes only through the hardness and persistence of life. Ghana reminds us of that. You better get ready go to prison. When I looked out and saw the prime minister there with his prison cap on that night, that reminded me of that fact that freedom never comes easy. It comes through hard labor and it comes through toil. It comes through hours of despair and disappointment.

And that's the way it goes. There is no crown without a cross. I wish we could get to Easter without going to Good Friday, but history tells us that we got to go by Good Friday before we can get to Easter. That's the long story of freedom, isn't it? Before you get to Canaan you've got a Red Sea to confront. You have a hardened heart of a pharaoh to confront. You have the prodigious hilltops of evil in the wilderness to confront. And even when you get up to the Promised Land, you have giants in the land. The beautiful thing about it is that there are a few people who've been over in the land. They have spied enough to say, "Even though the giants are there we can possess the land, because we got the internal fiber to stand up amid anything we have to face."

The road to freedom is a difficult, hard road. It always makes for temporary setbacks. And those people who tell you today that there is more tension in Montgomery than there has ever been are telling you right. Whenever you get out of Egypt, you always confront a little tension, you always confront a little temporary setback. If you didn't confront that you'd never get out. You must remember that the tensionless period that we like to think of was the period when the Negro was complacently adjusted to segregation, discrimination, insult and exploitation. And the period of tension is the period when the Negro has decided to rise up and break aloose from that. And this is the peace that we are seeking: not an old negative obnoxious peace which is merely the absence of tension, but a positive, lasting peace, which is the presence of brotherhood and justice. And it is never brought about without this temporary period of tension.

The road to freedom is difficult, but finally, Ghana tells us that the forces of the universe are on the side of justice. That is what it tells us, now. You can interpret Ghana any kind of way you want to, but Ghana tells me that the forces of the universe are on the side of justice. That night when I saw that old flag coming down and the new flag coming up, I saw something else. That wasn't just an ephemeral, evanescent event appearing on the stage of history. But it was an event with eternal meaning, for it symbolizes something. That thing symbolized to me that an old order is passing away and a new order is coming into being. An old order of colonialism, of segregation, of discrimination is passing away now. And a new order of justice and freedom and goodwill is being born. That's what it said. Somehow the forces of justice stand on the side of the universe, and that you can't ultimately trample over God's children and profit by it.

I want to come back to Montgomery now, but I must stop by London for a moment. For London reminds me of something. I never will forget the day we went into London. The next day we started moving around this great city, the only city in the world that is almost as large as New York City. Over eight million people in London, about eight million, three hundred thousand; New York about eight million, five hundred thousand. London is larger in area than New York, though. Standing in London is an amazing picture. And I never will forget the experience I had, the thoughts that came to my mind. When we went to Buckingham Palace. And I looked there at all of Britain, at all of the pomp and circumstance of royalty. And I thought about all of the queens and kings that had passed through here. Look at the beauty of the changing of the guards and all of the guards with their beautiful horses. It's a beautiful sight. Move on from there and go over to Parliament. Move into the House of Lords and the House of Commons. There with all of its beauty standing up before the world is one of the most beautiful sights in the world.

Then I remember, we went on over to Westminster Abbey. And I thought about several things when we went in this great church, this great cathedral, the center of the Church of England. We walked around and went to the tombs of the kings and queens buried there. Most of the kings and queens of England are buried right there in the Westminster Abbey. And I walked around. On the one hand I enjoyed and appreciated the great gothic architecture of that massive cathedral. I stood there in awe thinking about the greatness of God and man's feeble attempt to reach up for God. And I thought something else. I thought about the Church of England. My mind went back to Buckingham Palace, and I said that this is the symbol of a dying system. There was a day that the queens and kings of England could boast that the sun never sets on the British Empire. A day when she occupied the greater portion of Australia, the greater portion of Canada. There was a day when she ruled most of China, most of Africa, and all of India. I started thinking about this empire.

I started thinking about the fact that she ruled over India one day. Mahatma Gandhi stood there at every hand, trying to get the freedom of his people. And they never bowed to it. They never, they decided that they were going to stand up and hold India in humiliation and in colonialism many, many years. I remember we passed by Ten Downing Street. That's the place where the prime minister of England lives. And I remember that a few years ago a man lived there by the name of Winston Churchill. One day he stood up before the world and said, "I did not become His Majesty's first minister to preside over the liquidation of the British Empire."

And I thought about the fact that a few weeks ago a man by the name of Anthony Eden lived there. And out of all of his knowledge of the Middle East, he decided to rise up and march his armies with the forces of Israel and France into Egypt. And there they confronted their doom, because they were revolting against world opinion. Egypt, a little country. Egypt, a country with no military power. They could have easily defeated Egypt. But they did not realize that they were fighting more than Egypt. They were attacking world opinion, they were fighting the whole Asian-African bloc, which is the bloc that now thinks and moves and determines the course of the history of the world.

I thought of many things. I thought of the fact that the British Empire exploited India. Think about it! A nation with four hundred million people and the British exploited them so much that out of a population of four hundred million, three hundred and fifty million made an annual income of less than fifty dollars a year. Twenty-five of that had to be used for taxes and the other things of life. I thought about dark Africa. And how the people there, if they can make a hundred dollars a year, they are living very well they think. Two shillings a day—one shilling is fourteen cents; two shillings, twenty-eight cents—that's a good wage. That's because of the domination of the British Empire.

All of these things came to my mind, and when I stood there in Westminster Abbey, with all of its beauty, and I thought about all of the beautiful hymns and anthems that the people would go in there to sing. And yet the Church of England never took a stand against this system. The Church of England sanctioned it. The Church of England gave it moral stature. All of the exploitation perpetuated by the British Empire was sanctioned by the Church of England.

But something else came to my mind. God comes in the picture even when the Church won't take a stand. God has injected a principle in this universe. God has said that all men must respect the dignity and worth of all human personality, "And if you don't do that, I will take charge!" It seems this morning that I can hear God speaking. I can hear Him speaking throughout the universe saying, "Be still and know that I am God. And if you don't stop, if you don't straighten up, if you don't stop exploiting people, I'm going to rise up and break the backbone of your power. And your power will be no more!" And the power of Great Britain is no more. I looked at France. I looked at Britain. And I thought about the Britain that could boast, "The sun never sets on our great Empire." And I say now she had gone to the level that the sun hardly rises on the British Empire. Because it was based on exploitation. Because the God of the universe eventually takes a stand.

And I say to you this morning, my friends, rise up and know that as you struggle for justice, you do not struggle alone. But God struggles with you. And He's working every day. Somehow I can look out, I can look out across the seas and across the universe, and cry out "Mine eyes have seen the glory of the coming of the Lord. He is trampling out the vintage where the grapes of wrath are stored." Then I think about it because His truth is marching on, and I can sing another chorus: "Hallelujah, glory hallelujah! His truth is marching on."

Then I can hear Isaiah again, because it has profound meaning to me, that somehow "every valley shall be exalted, and every hill shall be made low; the crooked places shall be made straight, and the rough places plain; and the glory of the Lord shall be revealed, and all flesh shall see it together."

That's the beauty of this thing: all flesh shall see it together. Not some from the heights of Park Street and others from the dungeons of slum areas. Not some from the pinnacles of the British Empire and some from the dark deserts of Africa. Not some from inordinate, superfluous wealth and others from abject, deadening poverty. Not some white and not some black, not some yellow and not some brown, but all flesh shall see it together. They shall see it from Montgomery. They shall see it from New York. They shall see it from Ghana. They shall see it from China.

For I can look out and see a great number, as John saw, marching into the great eternity, because God is working in this world, and at this hour, and at this moment. And God grants that we will get on board and start marching with God because we got orders now to break down the bondage and the walls of colonialism, exploitation, and imperialism. To break them down to the point that no man will trample over another man, but that all men will respect the dignity and worth of all human personality. And then we will be in Canaan's freedom land.

Moses might not get to see Canaan, but his children will see it. He even got to the mountain top enough to see it and that assured him that it was coming. But the beauty of the thing is that there's always Joshua to take up his work and take the children on in. And it's there waiting with its milk and honey, and with all of the bountiful beauty that God has in store for His children. Oh, what exceedingly marvelous things God has in store for us. Grant that we will follow Him enough to gain them.

[recording interrupted] O, God, our gracious Heavenly Father, help us to see the insights that come from this new nation. Help us to follow Thee and all of Thy creative works in this world. And that somehow we will discover that we are made to live together as brothers. And that it will come in this generation: the day when all men will recognize the fatherhood of God and the brotherhood of man. Amen.

"Introduction to Southwest Africa: The U.N.'s Stepchild"

Statement by Martin Luther King, Jr.
Published by the American
Committee on Africa (ACOA)

OCTOBER 1959

———◇◇◇———

Africa is today a continent in transition. It is the land in which a great social revolution is taking place. You can hear the deep rumbling of this from the Sahara Desert to the Cape of Good Hope. Africans are united in their deep yearning for freedom and human dignity. They are determined to end the exploitation of their lives and to have a full share in their own future and destiny. The story of this struggle for freedom and independence is a familiar one. It has been told by every major American periodical and dramatized on practically every television channel. It is the theme of numerous speeches and the subject of many fireside discussions.

Despite this unusual coverage of African affairs, there are still areas in this vast and complex continent whose problems and conditions are little known to Americans. One such area is South West Africa. About the only thing most of us Americans know about South West Africa is its geographical location in the emerging continent; northwest of apartheid.

This tragic land for many years was a German colony. After World War I it was a League of Nations mandate under the Union of South Africa. After World War II and the demise of the League, South Africa tried to annex South West Africa. The League's legal successor—the United Nations—so far has prevented this action. The U.N. has not, however, yet been able to prevent South Africa from treating the Africans in this territory with the same regime of oppression and segregation as it gives the non-whites in its own territory.

While Christianity has been timid in too much of Africa, I am glad that Michael Scott—a clergyman—for more than a decade has represented the Herero people of South West Africa when South Africa refused to allow their representatives to appear before the U.N. Now two or three residents have managed to tell the U.N. their own story. It is not a pleasant story. At places, it has a nightmarish effect and points up some of the most tragic expressions of man's inhumanity to man. It is the story of more than 450,000 people constantly being trampled over by the iron feet of injustice.

This is the story the American people should know—one which their delegates at the U.N. should act upon. If for no other reason, we should know this story and act upon it because injustice anywhere is a threat to justice everywhere.

"My Talk with Ben Bella"

Statement by Martin Luther King, Jr.

New York Amsterdam News

NEW YORK, NEW YORK, OCTOBER 27, 1962

—◆◇◆—

A few days ago I had the good fortune of talking with Premier Ben Bella of the new Algerian Republic. Algeria is one of the most recent African nations to remove the last sanction of colonialism. For almost two hours Mr. Ben Bella and I discussed issues ranging from the efficacy of nonviolence to the Cuban crisis. However, it was on the question of racial injustice that we spent most of our time. As I sat talking with Mr. Ben Bella he displayed again and again an intimate knowledge of the Negro struggle here in America. The details of the Montgomery bus protest were immediately at his fingertips. He understood clearly what the issues were. The "Sit-ins" of 1960 were discussed animatedly and he expressed regret at the violence that accompanied the Freedom Rides. He knew all about Albany, Georgia, too, and Oxford, Mississippi was currently in the headlines. The significance of our conversation was Ben Bella's complete familiarity with the progression of events in the Negro struggle for full citizenship.

Our nation needs to note this well. All through our talks he repeated or inferred, "We are brothers." For Ben Bella, it was unmistakably clear that there is a close relationship between colonialism and segregation. He perceived that both are immoral systems aimed at the degradation of human personality. The battle of the Algerians against colonialism and the battle of the Negro against segregation is a common struggle. This points up a sobering fact for our nation. The matter of racial segregation in America has international implications. Either we must solve our human relations dilemma occasioned by race and color prejudice—and solve it soon—or we shall lose our moral and political voice in the world community of nations. *Ben Bella said this!* Racism in our nation must go or we will be relegated to a second-rate power in the world. We must face the inescapable fact that the shape of the world today does not afford us the luxury of an anemic democracy. The price that America must pay for the continued oppression of the Negro is the price of its own destruction. I must hasten to say, however, that this is not the only reason that America must solve this cancerous, domestic problem.

It must not be done merely to meet the Communist challenge; it must not be done merely to appeal to Asian and African peoples; in the final analysis, equal opportunity without regard to race must be established in America *because it is right.*

The Mississippi debacle of a few days ago pointed up this sore need in our midst. Somewhere in our ranks of government, education, the church and business, strong, clear voices must be raised to declare that integration in American life is to be effected, not alone because it is the law of the land or to keep our good name, but because it is a moral demand of the universe. Men and women all over America must be reminded over and over again that racial segregation is morally wrong because it relegates persons to the status of things.

"The Negro Looks at Africa"

Statement by Martin Luther King, Jr.

New York Amsterdam News

NEW YORK, NEW YORK, DECEMBER 8, 1962

———◇◇◇———

This past week-end might be considered monumental in the life of the American Negro. More than one hundred conferees gathered at the Arden House Campus of Columbia University at Harriman, New York to consider the relationship of the new independent nations of Africa and the black community of this nation. The great significance of the conference was not the assembling of these people who constitute the major and minor facets of Negro life in America alone; rather it was the *purpose* for which they met which attaches such great significance to the Arden House Conference: The American Negro's growing awareness of his world citizenship is an earmark of his developing maturity! That such an imposing array of leadership representative of the broad base of the Negro community should concern itself with its relevant role in taking a look at America's foreign policy as it relates to the emergent nations in Africa belies the fact that the strides we have made as a minority community here at home have brought with it a healthy break with provincialism that allows us to be concerned beyond what happens on 125th Street in New York or Beale Street in Memphis.

The conference was jointly sponsored by organizations identified with civil rights, labor, fraternal or intergroup ties. It was formally named the American Negro Leadership Conference on Africa and the mechanics were heroically handled by Theodore Brown, former civil rights staffer of the AFL-CIO.

The Negro recognizes that he lives in a world community. There was a time when the intensity of our own problems excluded our awareness of the existence of injustice anywhere as a threat to justice everywhere.

Colonialism and segregation are nearly synonymous; they are children in the same family, for their common end is economic exploitation, political domination and the debasing of human personality. In many ways the future of the emergent African nations (particularly those below the Sahara) and the American Negro are intertwined. As long as segregation and discrimination exist in our nation, the longer the chances of survival are for colonialism and *vice-versa,* for the very same set of complex politico-economic forces are operative in both instances. There seems always the choice between political expediency and that which is morally compelling, or the choice between advantageous economic aid and military alliances versus the establishment of racial and political justice.

It is tragic that our foreign policy on Africa is so ambivalent; for example, on the one hand, we decry in some mild manner the apartheid policy of the Union of South Africa but economically we continue "business-as-usual" in spite of the stringent racist policies being enforced and intensified. We do not support economic sanctions in the United Nations though we impose them ourselves.

One of the means by which we could demonstrate sincerity of purpose is a broader use of Negro Americans in our diplomatic corps that serves the independent and emergent nations.

In a diplomatic corps of more than a hundred ambassadors, it is regrettable that there are only two Negroes. This represents no increase at all since the last Administration.

The current struggle to win the minds of men and nations to the free world will not be won militarily. The most significant thrust will be the launching of a moral offensive for freedom and justice. America must come to see that this is the most powerful weapon she can use to defeat the communist attempt to win the minds of the colored nations of the world. Unless our foreign policy toward colonially-dominated nations in Africa is drastically changed, we will not be able to use our moral influence along with other political and economic stratagems to thwart the inevitability of a bloodbath in the sub-Sahara African nations.

It is toward these noble ends that the focus of the Arden House Conference was directed. It is our hope that the American Negro Leadership Conference on Africa can play some meaningful role in shaping American foreign policy that will be consistent with our own democratic posture. This can be aided immeasurably by decisiveness in dealing with the dilemma of race and color prejudice here in America.

A strong functional attitude on the part of the present Administration against racism at home will consequently evolve a strong functional attitude against racism in our foreign policy. It is unthinkable that we can allow ourselves knowingly or *unknowingly* to be a party to continued political and economic domination of native Africans who so desperately need relief.

"Palm Sunday Sermon on Mohandas K. Gandhi"

Sermon by Martin Luther King, Jr.

Dexter Avenue Baptist Church

MONTGOMERY, ALABAMA, MARCH 22, 1959

———⟨⋄⟩———

To the cross and its significance in human experience. This is the time in the year when we think of the love of God breaking forth into time out of eternity. This is the time of the year when we come to see that the most powerful forces in the universe are not those forces of military might but those forces of spiritual might. And as we sing together this great hymn of our church, the Christian church, hymn number 191, let us think about it again:

> When I survey the wondrous cross,
> On which the prince of glory died,
> I count my richest gains but loss
> And pour contempt on all my pride.

A beautiful hymn. I think if there is any hymn of the Christian church that I would call a favorite hymn, it is this one. And then it goes on to say, in that last stanza:

> Were the whole realm of nature mine,
> That was a present far too small.
> Love so amazing, so divine,
> Demands my life, my all and my all.

We think about Christ and the cross in the days ahead as he walks through Jerusalem and he's carried from Jerusalem to Calvary Hill, where he is crucified. Let us think of this wondrous cross. [*Congregation sings "When I Survey the Wondrous Cross"*]

83

This, as you know, is what has traditionally been known in the Christian church as Palm Sunday. And ordinarily the preacher is expected to preach a sermon on the Lordship or the Kingship of Christ—the triumphal entry, or something that relates to this great event as Jesus entered Jerusalem, for it was after this that Jesus was crucified. And I remember, the other day, at about seven or eight days ago, standing on the Mount of Olives and looking across just a few feet and noticing that gate that still stands there in Jerusalem, and through which Christ passed into Jerusalem, into the old city. The ruins of that gate stand there, and one feels the sense of Christ's mission as he looks at the gate. And he looks at Jerusalem, and he sees what could take place in such a setting. And you notice there also the spot where the temple stood, and it was here that Jesus passed and he went into the temple and ran the money-changers out.

And so that, if I talked about that this morning, I could talk about it not only from what the Bible says but from personal experience, first-hand experience. But I beg of you to indulge me this morning to talk about the life of a man who lived in India. And I think I'm justified in doing this because I believe this man, more than anybody else in the modern world, caught the spirit of Jesus Christ and lived it more completely in his life. His name was Gandhi, Mohandas K. Gandhi. And after he lived a few years, the poet Tagore, who lived in India, gave him another name: "Mahatma," the great soul. And we know him as Mahatma Gandhi.

I would like to use a double text for what I have to say this morning, both of them are found in the gospel as recorded by Saint John. One found in the tenth chapter, and the sixteenth verse, and it reads, "I have other sheep, which are not of this fold." "I have other sheep, which are not of this fold." And then the other one is found in the fourteenth chapter of John, in the twelfth verse. It reads, "Verily, verily, I say unto you, he that believeth on me, the works that I do, shall he do also. And greater works than these shall he do because I go unto my Father."

I want you to notice these two passages of scripture. On the one hand, "I have other sheep that are not of this fold." I think

Jesus is saying here in substance that "I have followers who are not in this inner circle." He's saying in substance that "I have people dedicated and following my ways who have not become attached to the institution surrounding my name. I have other sheep that are not of this fold. And my influence is not limited to the institutional Christian church." I think this is what Jesus would say if he were living today concerning this passage, that "I have people who are following me who've never joined the Christian church as an institution."

And then that other passage, I think Jesus was saying this—it's a strange thing, and I used to wonder what Jesus meant when he said, "There will be people who will do greater things than I did." And I have thought about the glory and honor surrounding the life of Christ, and I thought about the fact that he represented the absolute revelation of God. And I've thought about the fact that in his life, he represented all of the glory of eternity coming into time. And how would it be possible for anybody to do greater works than Christ? How would it be possible for anybody even to match him, or even to approximate his work?

But I've come to see what Christ meant. Christ meant that in his life he would only touch a few people. And in his lifetime—and if you study the life of Christ, and if you know your Bible you realize that Christ never traveled outside of Palestine, and his influence in his own lifetime was limited to a small group of people. He never had more than twelve followers in his lifetime; others heard about him and others came to see him, but he never had but twelve real followers, and three of them turned out to be not too good. But he pictured the day that his spirit and his influence would go beyond the borders of Palestine, and that men would catch his message and carry it over the world, and that men all over the world would grasp the truth of his gospel. And they would be able to do things that he couldn't do. They were able, be able to travel places that he couldn't travel. And they would be able to convert people that he couldn't convert in his lifetime. And this is what he meant when he said, "Greater works shall ye do, for an Apostle Paul will catch my work."

And I remember just last Tuesday morning standing on that beautiful hill called the Acropolis in Athens. And there, standing around the Parthenon, as it stands still in all of its beautiful and impressive proportions, although it has been torn somewhat through wars, but it still stands there. And right across from the Acropolis you see Mars Hill. And I remember when our guide said, "That's the hill where the Apostle Paul preached."

Now when you think of the fact that Athens is a long ways from Jerusalem, for we traveled right over Damascus where Paul was converted, and Damascus is at least five hours by flight from Athens. And you think about the fact that Paul had caught this message and carried it beyond the Damascus Road all over the world, and he had gone as far as Greece, as far as Athens, to preach the gospel of Jesus Christ. This is what Jesus meant that "somebody will catch my message, and they would be able to carry it in places that I couldn't carry it, and they would be able to do things in their lives that I couldn't do."

And I believe these two passages of scripture apply more uniquely to the life and work of Mahatma Gandhi than to any other individual in the history of the world. For here was a man who was not a Christian in terms of being a member of the Christian church but who was a Christian. And it is one of the strange ironies of the modern world that the greatest Christian of the twentieth century was not a member of the Christian church. And the second thing is, that this man took the message of Jesus Christ and was able to do even greater works than Jesus did in his lifetime. Jesus himself predicted this: "Ye shall do even greater works."

Now let us look at the life, as briefly as possible, the life of this man and his work, and see just what it gives us, and what this life reveals to us in terms of the struggles ahead. I would say the first thing that we must see about this life is that Mahatma Gandhi was able to achieve for his people independence through nonviolent means. I think you should underscore this. He was able to achieve for his people independence from the domination of the British Empire without lifting one gun or without uttering one curse word. He did it with the spirit of Jesus Christ in his heart and the love of God, and this was all he had. He had no weapons. He had no army, in terms of military might. And yet he was able to achieve independence from the largest empire in the history of this world without picking up a gun or without any ammunition. Gandhi was born in India in a little place called Porbandar, down almost in central India. And he had seen the conditions of this country. India had been under the domination of the British Empire for many years. And under the domination of the British Empire, the people of India suffered all types of exploitation. And you think about the fact that while Britain was in India, that out of a population of four hundred million people, more than three hundred and sixty-five million of these people made less than fifty dollars a year. And more than half of this had to be spent for taxes.

Gandhi looked at all of this. He looked at his people as they lived in ghettos and hovels and as they lived out on the streets, many of them. And even today, after being exploited so many years, they haven't been able to solve those problems. For we landed in Bombay, India, and I never will forget it, that night. We got up early in the morning to take a plane for Delhi. And as we rode out to the airport we looked out on the street and saw people sleeping out on the sidewalks and out in the streets, and everywhere we went to. Walk through the train station, and you can't hardly get to the train, because people are sleeping on the platforms of the train station. No homes to live in. In Bombay, India, where they have a population of three million people, five hundred thousand of these people sleep on the streets at night. Nowhere to sleep, no homes to live in, making no more than fifteen or twenty dollars a year or even less than that.

And this was the exploitation that Mahatma Gandhi noticed years ago. And even more than that, these people were humiliated and embarrassed and segregated in their own land. There were places that the Indian people could not even go in their own land. The British had come in there and set up clubs and other places and even hotels where Indians couldn't even enter in their own land. Gandhi looked at all of this, and as a young lawyer, after he had just left England and gotten his law—received his law training, he went over to South Africa. And there he saw in South Africa, and Indians were even exploited there.

And one day he was taking a train to Pretoria, and he had first-class accommodations on that train. And when they came to pick up the tickets they noticed that he was an Indian, that he had a brown face, and they told him to get out and move on to the third-class accommodation, that he wasn't supposed to be there with any first-class accommodation. And Gandhi that day refused to move, and they threw him off the train. And there, in that cold station that night, he stayed all night, and he started meditating on his plight and the plight of his people. And he decided from that point on that he would never submit himself to injustice, or to exploitation.

It was there on the next day that he called a meeting of all of the Indians in South Africa, in that particular region of South Africa, and told them what had happened, and told them what was happening to them every day, and said that, "We must do something about it. We must organize ourselves to rid our community, the South African community, and also the Indian community back home, of the domination and the exploitation of foreign powers."

But Mahatma Gandhi came to something else in that moment. As he started organizing his forces in South Africa, he read the Sermon on the Mount. He later read the works of the American poet Thoreau. And he later read the Russian author Tolstoy. And he found something in all of this that gave him insights. Started reading in the Bible, "turn the other cheek," "resist evil with good," "blessed are the meek, for they shall inherit the earth." And all of these things inspired him to no end. He read Thoreau as he said that no just man can submit to anything evil, even if it means standing up and being disobedient to the laws of the state. And so this he combined into a new method, and he said to his people, "Now, it's possible to resist evil; this is your first responsibility; never adjust to evil, resist it. But if you can resist it without resorting to violence or to hate, you can stand up against it and still love the individuals that carry on the evil system that you are resisting." And a few years later, after he won a victory in South Africa, he went back to India. And there his people called on him, called on his leadership, to organize them and get ready for the trials ahead, and he did just that. He went back, and in 1917 he started his first campaign in India. And throughout his long struggle there, he followed the way of nonviolent resistance. Never uttered a curse word, mark you. He never owned an instrument of violence. And he had nothing but love and understanding goodwill in his heart for the people who were seeking to defeat him and who were exploiting and humiliating his people.

And then came that day when he said to the people of India, "I'm going to leave this community." He had set up in a place called Ahmadabad, and there was the Sabarmati ashram. He lived there with a group of people; his ashram was a place of quiet and meditation where the people lived together. And one day he said to those people, "I'm going to leave this place, and I will not return until India has received her independence." And this was in 1930. And he had so organized the whole of India then; people had left their jobs. People with tremendous and powerful law practices had left their jobs. The president of India was a lawyer who had made almost a million rupees—a million dollars—and he left it, turned it all over to the movement. The father, the president of—the prime minister of India, Mr. Nehru, left his law practice to get in the freedom movement with Gandhi, and he had organized the whole of India.

And you have read of the Salt March, which was a very significant thing in the Indian struggle. And this demonstrates how Gandhi used this method of nonviolence and how he would mobilize his people and galvanize the whole of the nation to bring about victory. In India, the British people had come to the point where they were charging the Indian people a tax on all of the salt, and they would not allow them even to make their own salt from all of the salt seas around the country. They couldn't touch it; it was against the law. And Gandhi got all of the people of India to see the injustice of this. And he decided one day that they would march from Ahmadabad down to a place called Dandi.

We had the privilege of spending a day or so at Ahmadabad at that Sabarmati ashram, and we stood there at the point where Gandhi started his long walk of two hundred and eighteen miles. And he started there walking with eighty people. And gradually the number grew to a million, and it grew to millions and millions. And finally, they kept walking and walking until they reached the little village of Dandi. And there, Gandhi went on and reached down in the river, or in the sea rather, and brought up a little salt in his hand to demonstrate and dramatize the fact that they were breaking this law in protest against the injustices they had faced all over the years with these salt laws.

And Gandhi said to his people, "If you are hit, don't hit back; even if they shoot at you, don't shoot back; if they curse you, don't curse back, but just keep moving. Some of us might have to die before we get there; some of us might be thrown in jail before we get there, but let us just keep moving." And they kept moving, and they walked and walked, and millions of them had gotten together when they finally reached that point. And the British Empire knew, then, that this little man had mobilized the people of India to the point that they could never defeat them. And they realized, at that very point, that this was the beginning of the end of the British Empire as far as India was concerned.

He was able to mobilize and galvanize more people than, in his lifetime, than any other person in the history of this world. And just with a little love in his heart and understanding goodwill and a refusal to cooperate with an evil law, he was able to break the backbone of the British Empire. And this, I think, is one of the most significant things that has ever happened in the history of the world, and more than three hundred and ninety million people achieved their freedom. And they achieved it nonviolently when a man refused to follow the way of hate, and he refused to follow the way of violence, and only decided to follow the way of love and understanding goodwill and refused to cooperate with any system of evil.

And the significant thing is that when you follow this way, when the battle is almost over, and a new friendship and reconciliation exists between the people who have been the oppressors and the oppressed. There is no greater friendship anywhere in the world today than between the Indian people and the British people. If you ask the Indian people today who they love more, what people, whether they love Americans more, British more, they will say to you immediately that they love the British people more.

The night we had dinner with Prime Minister Nehru the person who sat at that dinner table with us, as a guest of the prime minister at that time, was Lady Mountbatten with her daughter, the wife of Lord Mountbatten, who was the viceroy of India when it received its independence. And they're marvelous and great and lasting friends. There is a lasting friendship there. And this is only because Gandhi followed the way of love and nonviolence, refusing to hate and refusing to follow the way of violence. And a new friendship exists. The aftermath of violence is always bitterness; the aftermath of nonviolence is the creation of the beloved community so that when the battle is over, it's over, and a new love and a new understanding and a new relationship comes into being between the oppressed and the oppressor.

This little man, one of the greatest conquerors that the world has ever known. Somebody said that when Mahatma Gandhi was coming over to England for the roundtable conference in 1932, a group of people stood there waiting. And somebody pointed out, and while they were waiting somebody said, "You see around that cliff? That was where Julius Caesar came, the way he came in when he invaded Britain years ago." And then somebody pointed over to another place and said, "That was the way William the Conqueror came in. They invaded years ago in the Battle of Hastings." Then somebody else looked over and said, "There is another conqueror coming in. In just a few minutes the third and greatest conqueror that has ever come into Great Britain." And strangely enough, this little man came in with no armies, no guards around him, no military might, no beautiful clothes, just loin cloth, but this man proved to be the greatest conqueror that the British Empire ever faced. He was able to achieve, through love and nonviolence, the independence of his people and break the backbone of the British Empire. "Ye shall do greater works than I have done." And this is exemplified in the life of Mahatma Gandhi.

Let me rush on to say a second thing: here is a man who achieved in his life absolute self-discipline. Absolute self-discipline. So that in his life there was no gulf between the private and the public; there was no gulf in his life between the "is" and the "oughts." Here was a man who had absolved the "isness" of his being and the "oughtness" of his being. And this was one of the greatest accomplishments in his life. Gandhi used to say to his people, "I have no secrets. My life is an open book." And he lived that every day. He achieved in his life absolute self-discipline.

He started out as a young lawyer. He went to South Africa, and he became a thriving, promising lawyer making more than thirty thousand dollars a year. And then he came to see that he had a task ahead to free his people. And he vowed poverty, decided to do away with all of the money that he had made, and he went back to India and started wearing the very clothes that all of these disinherited masses of people of India had been wearing. He had been a popular young man in England, worn all of the beautiful clothes and his wife the beautiful saris of India with all of its silk beauty, but then he came to that point of saying to his wife, "You've got to drop this." And he started wearing what was called the dhoti, loin cloth, the same thing that these masses of people wore. He did it, identified himself with them absolutely.

And he had no income; he had nothing in this world, not even a piece of property. This man achieved in his life absolute self-discipline to the point of renouncing the world. And when he died, the only thing that he owned was a pair of glasses, a pair of sandals, a loincloth, some false teeth, and some little monkeys who saw no evil, who said no evil, and who somehow didn't see any evil. This is all he had. And if you ask people in India today why was it that Mahatma Gandhi was able to do what he did in India, they would say they followed him because of his absolute sincerity and his absolute dedication. Here was a man who achieved in his life this bridging of the gulf between the "ought" and the "is." He achieved in his life absolute self-discipline.

And there is a final thing Mahatma Gandhi was able to do. He had the amazing capacity, the amazing capacity for internal criticism. Most others have the amazing capacity for external criticism. We can always see the evil in others; we can always see the evil in our oppressors. But Gandhi had the amazing capacity to see not only the splinter in his opponent's eye but also the planks in his own eye and the eye of his people. He had the amazing capacity for self-criticism. And this was true in his individual life; it was true in his family life; and it was true in his people's life. He not only criticized the British Empire, but he criticized his own people when they needed it, and he criticized himself when he needed it.

And whenever he made a mistake, he confessed it publicly. Here was a man who would say to his people, "I'm not perfect. I'm not infallible. I don't want you to start a religion around me. I'm not a god." And I'm convinced that today there would be a religion around Gandhi if Gandhi had not insisted all through his life that "I don't want a religion around me because I'm too human. I'm too fallible. Never think that I'm infallible."

And any time he made a mistake, even in his personal life or even in decisions that he made in the independence struggle, he came out in the public and said, "I made a mistake." In 1922, when he had started one of his first campaigns of nonviolence and some of the people started getting violent, some of the Indian people started getting violent, and they killed twenty some, twenty-eight of the British people in this struggle. And in the midst of this struggle, Gandhi came to the forefront of the scene and called the campaign off. And he stood up before the Indian people and before the British people and said, "I made a Himalayan blunder.

I thought my people were ready; I thought they were disciplined for this task." And people around Gandhi were angry with him. Even Prime Minister Nehru says in *Toward Freedom* that he was angry. His father was angry. All of these people who had left their hundreds and thousands of dollars to follow Gandhi and his movement were angry when he called this movement off. But he called it off because, as he said, "I've made a blunder." And he never hesitated to acknowledge before the public when he made a mistake. And he always went back and said, "I made a mistake. I'm going back to rethink it, I'm going back to meditate over it. And I'll be coming back. Don't think the struggle is over, don't think I'm retreating from this thing permanently and ultimately. I'm just taking a temporary retreat, because I made a mistake."

But not only that, he confessed the errors and the mistakes of his family. Even when his son, one of his sons, went wrong he wrote in his paper about it. And his wife committed an act once that was sinful to him. He had pledged himself to poverty, and he would never use any of the money that came in for his personal benefit. And one day his wife, feeling the need for some of that money that had come in, decided to use it. And Gandhi discovered it, and he wrote in his paper that his wife had committed a grave sin. He didn't mind letting the world know it. Here was a man who confessed his errors publicly and didn't mind if you saw him fail. He saw his own shortcomings, the shortcomings of his family, and then he saw the shortcomings of his own people.

We went in some little villages, and in these villages we saw hundreds of people sleeping on the ground. They didn't have any beds to sleep in. We looked in these same villages; there was no running water there, nothing to wash with. We looked in these villages, and we saw people there in their little huts and in their little rooms, and the cow, their little cow, or their calves slept in the same room with them. If they had a few chickens, the chickens slept in the same room with them. We looked at these people, and they had nothing that we would consider convenient, none of the comforts of life. Here they are, sleeping in the same room with the beast of the field. This is all they had. Pretty soon we discovered that these people were the untouchables.

Now you know in India you have what is known as the caste system, and that existed for years. And there were those people who were the outcasts, some seventy million of them. They were called untouchables. And these were the people who were exploited, and they were trampled over even by the Indian people themselves. And Gandhi looked at this system. Gandhi couldn't stand this system, and he looked at his people, and he said, "Now, you have selected me and you've asked me to free you from the political domination and the economic exploitation inflicted upon you by Britain. And here you are trampling over and exploiting seventy million of your brothers." And he decided that he would not ever adjust to that system and that he would speak against it and stand up against it the rest of his life.

And you read, back in his early life, the first thing he did when he went to India was to adopt an untouchable girl as his daughter. And his wife thought he was going crazy because she was a member of one of the high castes. And she said, "What in the world are you doing adopting an untouchable? We are not supposed to touch these people." And he said, "I am going to have this young lady as my daughter." And he brought her into his ashram, and she lived there, and she lives in India today. And he demonstrated in his own life that untouchability had to go. And one of the greatest tasks ever performed by Mahatma Gandhi was against untouchability.

One day he stood before his people and said, "You are exploiting these untouchables. Even though we are fighting with all that we have in our bodies and our souls to break loose from the bondage of the British Empire, we are exploiting these people, and we're taking from them their selfhood and their self-respect." And he said, "We will not even allow these people to go into temple." They couldn't go in the temple and worship God like other people. They could not draw water like other people, and there were certain streets they couldn't even walk on.

And he looked at all of this. One day he said, "Beginning on the twenty-first of September at twelve o'clock, I will refuse to eat. And I will not eat any more until the leaders of the caste system will come to me with the leaders of the untouchables and say that there will be an end to untouchability. And I will not eat any more until the Hindu temples of India will open their doors to the untouchables." And he refused to eat. And days passed. Nothing happened. Finally, when Gandhi was about to breathe his last, breathe his last breath and his body—it was all but gone and he had lost many pounds. A group came to him. A group from the untouchables and a group from the Brahmin caste came to him and signed a statement saying that we will no longer adhere to the caste system and to untouchability. And the priests of the temple came to him and said now the temple will be open unto the untouchables. And that afternoon, untouchables from all over India went into the temples, and all of these thousands and millions of people put their arms around the Brahmins and peoples of other castes. Hundreds and millions of people who had never touched each other for two thousand years were now singing and praising God together. And this was the great contribution that Mahatma Gandhi brought about.

And today in India, untouchability is a crime punishable by the law. And if anybody practices untouchability, he can be put in prison for as long as three years. And as one political leader said to me, "You cannot find in India one hundred people today who would sign the public statement endorsing untouchability." Here was a man who had the amazing capacity for internal criticism to the point that he saw the shortcomings of his own people. And he was just as firm against doing something about that as he was about doing away with the exploitation of the British Empire. And this is what makes him one of the great men of history.

And the final thing that I would like to say to you this morning is that the world doesn't like people like Gandhi. That's strange, isn't it? They don't like people like Christ. They don't like people like Abraham Lincoln. They kill them. And this man, who had done all of that for India, this man who had given his life and who had mobilized and galvanized four hundred million people for independence so that in 1947 India received its independence, and he became the father of that nation. This same man because he decided that he would not rest until he saw the Muslims and the Hindus together; they had been fighting among themselves, they had been in riots among themselves, and he wanted to see this straight. And one of his own fellow Hindus felt that he was a little too favorable toward the Muslims, felt that he was giving in a little too much toward the Muslims.

And one afternoon, when he was at Birla House, living there with one of the big industrialists for a few days in Delhi, he walked out to his evening prayer meeting. Every evening he had a prayer meeting where hundreds of people came, and he prayed with them. And on his way out there that afternoon, one of his fellow Hindus shot him. And here was a man of nonviolence, falling at the hand of a man of violence. Here was a man of love falling at the hands of a man of hate. This seems the way of history.

And isn't it significant that he died on the same day that Christ died; it was on a Friday. This is the story of history. But thank God it never stops here. Thank God Good Friday is never the end. And the man who shot Gandhi only shot him into the hearts of humanity. And just as when Abraham Lincoln was shot—mark you, for the same reason that Mahatma Gandhi was shot, that is, the attempt to heal the wounds of a divided nation. When the great leader Abraham Lincoln was shot, Secretary Stanton stood by the body of this leader and said, "Now he belongs to the ages." And that same thing can be said about Mahatma Gandhi now. He belongs to the ages, and he belongs especially to this age, an age drifting once more to its doom. And he has revealed to us that we must learn to go another way.

For in a day when Sputniks and Explorers are dashing through outer space and guided ballistic missiles are carving highways of death through the stratosphere, no nation can win a war. Today it is no longer a choice between violence and nonviolence; it is either nonviolence or nonexistence. It may not be that Mahatma Gandhi is God's appeal to this age, an age drifting to its doom. And that warning, and that appeal is always in the form of a warning: "He who lives by the sword will perish by the sword." Jesus said it years ago. Whenever men follow that and see that way, new horizons begin to emerge and a new world unfolds. Who today will follow Christ in his way and follow it so much that we'll be able to do greater things even than he did because we will be able to bring about the peace of the world and mobilize hundreds and thousands of men to follow the way of Christ?

I close by quoting the words of John Oxenham:

To every man there openeth a way, and ways, and a way
The high soul climbs the high way, and the low soul
    gropes the low,
And in between on the misty flats, the rest drift to and fro.
But to every man—to every nation, to every civilization—
    there openeth a high and a low way.
Every soul decideth which way it shall go.

And God grant that we shall choose the high way, even if it will mean assassination, even if it will mean crucifixion, for by going this way we will discover that death would be only the beginning of our influence.

"I have other sheep," says Jesus, "which are not of this fold. And if you will believe in me and follow my way, you will be even, you will be able to do even greater works than I did in my lifetime."

O God, our gracious Heavenly Father, we thank Thee for the fact that you have inspired men and women in all nations and in all cultures. We call you different names: some call Thee Allah; some call you Elohim; some call you Jehovah; some call you Brahma; and some call you the Unmoved Mover; some call you the Architectonic Good. But we know that these are all names for one and the same God, and we know you are one.

And grant, O God, that we will follow Thee and become so committed to Thy way and Thy kingdom that we will be able to establish in our lives and in this world a brotherhood. We will be able to establish here a kingdom of understanding, where men will live together as brothers and respect the dignity and worth of all human personality.

In the name and spirit of Jesus we pray. Amen.

We open the doors of the church now. Is there one who will accept the Christ this morning just as you are? Who will make that decision as we stand and sing together? One hundred and sixty-two.

Let us remain standing now for the recessional hymn. We are grateful to God for these persons who have come to unite with the church.

"My Trip to the Land of Gandhi"

Article by Martin Luther King, Jr.

Ebony

JULY 1959

———◇◇◇———

For a long time I had wanted to take a trip to India. Even as a child the entire Orient held a strange fascination for me—the elephants, the tigers, the temples, the snake charmers and all the other storybook characters.

While the Montgomery boycott was going on, India's Gandhi was the guiding light of our technique of non-violent social change. We spoke of him often. So as soon as our victory over bus segregation was won, some of my friends said: "Why don't you go to India and see for yourself what the Mahatma, whom you so admire, has wrought."

In 1956 when Pandit Jawaharlal Nehru, India's Prime Minister, made a short visit to the United States, he was gracious enough to say that he wished that he and I had met and had his diplomatic representatives make inquiries as to the possibility of my visiting his country some time soon. Our former American ambassador to India, Chester Bowles, wrote me along the same lines.

But every time that I was about to make the trip, something would interfere. At one time it was my visit by prior commitment to Ghana. At another time my publishers were pressing me to finish writing *Stride Toward Freedom*. Then along came Mrs. Izola Ware Curry. When she struck me with that Japanese letter opener on that Saturday afternoon in September as I sat autographing books in a Harlem store, she not only knocked out the travel plans that I had but almost everything else as well.

After I recovered from this near-fatal encounter and was finally released by my doctors, it occurred to me that it might be better to get in the trip to India before plunging too deeply once again into the sea of the Southern segregation struggle.

I preferred not to take this long trip alone and asked my wife and my friend, Lawrence Reddick, to accompany me. Coretta was particularly interested in the women of India and Dr. Reddick in the history and government of that great country. He had written my biography, *Crusader Without Violence,* and said that my true test would come when the people who knew Gandhi looked me over and passed judgment upon me and the Montgomery movement. The three of us made up a sort of 3-headed team with six eyes and six ears for looking and listening.

The Christopher Reynolds Foundation made a grant through the American Friends Service Committee to cover most of the expenses of the trip and the Southern Christian Leadership Conference and the Montgomery Improvement Association added their support. The Gandhi Memorial Trust of India extended an official invitation, through diplomatic channels, for our visit.

And so on February 3, 1959, just before midnight, we left New York by plane. En route we stopped in Paris with Richard Wright, an old friend of Reddick's, who brought us up to date on European attitudes on the Negro question and gave us a taste of the best French cooking.

We missed our plane connection in Switzerland because of fog, arriving in India after a roundabout route, two days late. But from the time we came down out of the clouds at Bombay on February 10, until March 10, when we waved goodbye at the New Delhi airport, we had one of the [most] concentrated and eye-opening experiences of our lives. There is so much to tell that I can only touch upon a few of the high points.

At the outset, let me say that we had a grand reception in India. The people showered upon us the most generous hospitality imaginable. We were graciously received by the Prime Minister, the President and the Vice-President of the nation; members of Parliament, Governors and Chief Ministers of various Indian states; writers, professors, social reformers and at least one saint.

Since our pictures were in the newspapers very often it was not unusual for us to be recognized by crowds in public places and on public conveyances. Occasionally I would take a morning walk in the large cities, and out of the most unexpected places someone would emerge and ask: "Are you Martin Luther King?"

Virtually every door was open to us. We had hundreds of invitations that the limited time did not allow us to accept. We were looked upon as brothers with the color of our skins as something of an asset. But the strongest bond of fraternity was the common cause of minority and colonial peoples in America, Africa and Asia struggling to throw off racialism and imperialism.

We had the opportunity to share our views with thousands of Indian people through endless conversations and numerous discussion sessions. I spoke before university groups and public meetings all over India. Because of the keen interest that the Indian people have in the race problem these meetings were usually packed. Occasionally interpreters were used, but on the whole I spoke to audiences that understood English.

The Indian people love to listen to the Negro spirituals. Therefore, Coretta ended up singing as much as I lectured. We discovered that autograph seekers are not confined to America. After appearances in public meetings and while visiting villages we were often besieged for autographs. Even while riding planes, more than once pilots came into the cabin from the cockpit requesting our signatures.

We got a good press throughout our stay. Thanks to the Indian papers, the Montgomery bus boycott was already well known in that country. Indian publications perhaps gave a better continuity of our 381-day bus strike than did most of our papers in the United States. Occasionally I meet some American fellow citizen who even now asks me how the bus boycott is going, apparently never having read that our great day of bus integration, December 21, 1956, closed that chapter of our history.

We held press conferences in all of the larger cities—Delhi, Calcutta, Madras and Bombay—and talked with newspaper men almost everywhere we went. They asked sharp questions and at

times appeared to be hostile but that was just their way of bringing out the story that they were after. As reporters, they were
scrupulously fair with us and in their editorials showed an amazing grasp of what was going on in America and other parts of
the world.

The trip had a great impact upon me personally. It was wonderful to be in Gandhi's land, to talk with his son, his grand-
sons, his cousin and other relatives; to share the reminiscences
of his close comrades; to visit his ashrama, to see the countless
memorials for him and finally to lay a wreath on his entombed
ashes at Rajghat. I left India more convinced than ever before that
non-violent resistance is the most potent weapon available to oppressed people in their struggle for freedom. It was a marvelous
thing to see the amazing results of a non-violent campaign. The
aftermath of hatred and bitterness that usually follows a violent
campaign was found nowhere in India. Today a mutual friendship based on complete equality exists between the Indian and
British people within the commonwealth. The way of acquies-
cence leads to moral and spiritual suicide. The way of violence
leads to bitterness in the survivors and brutality in the destroyers.
But, the way of non-violence leads to redemption and the creation
of the beloved community.

The spirit of Gandhi is very much alive in India today. Some of
his disciples have misgivings about this when they remember the
drama of the fight for national independence and when they look
around and find nobody today who comes near the stature of the
Mahatma. But any objective observer must report that Gandhi is
not only the greatest figure in India's history but that his influence
is felt in almost every aspect of life and public policy today. India can never forget Gandhi. For example, the Gandhi Memorial
Trust (also known as the Gandhi Smarak Nidhi) collected some
$130 million soon after the death of "the father of the nation."
This was perhaps the largest, spontaneous, mass monetary contribution to the memory of a single individual in the history of the
world. This fund, along with support from the Government and
other institutions, is resulting in the spread and development of

Gandhian philosophy, the implementing of his constructive program, the erection of libraries and the publication of works by and about the life and times of Gandhi. Posterity could not escape him even if it tried. By all standards of measurement, he is one of the half dozen greatest men in world history.

I was delighted that the Gandhians accepted us with open arms. They praised our experiment with the non-violent resistance technique at Montgomery. They seem to look upon it as an outstanding example of the possibilities of its use in western civilization. To them as to me it also suggests that non-violent resistance *when planned and positive in action* can work effectively even under totalitarian regimes.

We argued this point at some length with the groups of African students who are today studying in India. They felt that non-violent resistance could only work in a situation where the resisters had a potential ally in the conscience of the opponent. We soon discovered that they, like many others, tended to confuse passive resistance with non-resistance. This is completely wrong. True non-violent resistance is not unrealistic submission to evil power. It is rather a courageous confrontation of evil by the power of love, in the faith that it is better to be the recipient of violence than the inflictor of it, since the latter only multiplies the existence of violence and bitterness in the universe, while the former may develop a sense of shame in the opponent, and thereby bring about a transformation and change of heart.

Non-violent resistance does call for love, but it is not a sentimental love. It is a very stern love that would organize itself into collective action to right a wrong by taking on itself suffering. While I understand the reasons why oppressed people often turn to violence in their struggle for freedom, it is my firm belief that the crusade for independence and human dignity that is now reaching a climax in Africa will have a more positive effect on the world, if it is waged along the lines that were first demonstrated in that continent by Gandhi himself.

India is a vast country with vast problems. We flew over the long stretches, from North to South, East to West; took trains for shorter jumps and used automobiles and jeeps to get us into the less accessible places.

India is about a third the size of the United States but has almost three times as many people. Everywhere we went we saw crowded humanity—on the roads, in the city streets and squares, even in the villages.

Most of the people are poor and poorly dressed. The average income per person is less than $70 per year. Nevertheless, their turbans for their heads, loose flowing, wrap-around *dhotis* that they wear instead of trousers and the flowing saris that the women wear instead of dresses are colorful and picturesque. Many Indians wear part native and part western dress.

We think that we in the United States have a big housing problem but in the city of Bombay, for example, over a half million people sleep out of doors every night. These are mostly unattached, unemployed or partially employed males. They carry their bedding with them like foot soldiers and unroll it each night in any unoccupied space they can find—on the sidewalk, in a railroad station or at the entrance of a shop that is closed for the evening.

The food shortage is so widespread that it is estimated that less than 30% of the people get what we would call three square meals a day. During our great depression of the 1930's, we spoke of "a third of a nation" being "ill-housed, ill clad and ill fed." For India today, simply change one third to two thirds in that statement and that would make it about right.

As great as is unemployment, under-employment is even greater. Seventy per cent of the Indian people are classified as agricultural workers and most of these do less than 200 days of farm labor per year because of the seasonal fluctuations and other uncertainties of mother nature. Jobless men roam the city streets.

Great ills flow from the poverty of India but strangely there is relatively little crime. Here is another concrete manifestation of the wonderful spiritual quality of the Indian people. They are poor, jammed together and half starved but they do not take it out on each other. They are a kindly people. They do not abuse each other—verbally or physically—as readily as we do. We saw but one fist fight in India during our stay.

In contrast to the poverty-stricken, there are Indians who are rich, have luxurious homes, landed estates, fine clothes and show evidence of over-eating. The bourgeoise—white, black or brown—behaves about the same the world over.

And then there is, even here, the problem of segregation. We call it race in America; they call it caste in India. In both places it means that some are considered inferior, treated as though they deserve less.

We were surprised and delighted to see that India has made greater progress in the fight against caste "untouchability" than we have made here in our own country against race segregation. Both nations have federal laws against discrimination (acknowledging, of course, that the decision of our Supreme Court is the law of our land). But after this has been said, we must recognize that there are great differences between what India has done and what we have done on a problem that is very similar. The leaders of India have placed their moral power behind their law. From the Prime Minister down to the village councilmen, everybody declares publicly that untouchability is wrong. But in the United States some of our highest officials decline to render a moral judgment on segregation and some from the South publicly boast of their determination to maintain segregation. This would be unthinkable in India.

Moreover, Gandhi not only spoke against the caste system but he acted against it. He took "untouchables" by the hand and led them into the temples from which they had been excluded. To equal that, President Eisenhower would take a Negro child by the hand and lead her into Central High School in Little Rock.

Gandhi also renamed the untouchables, calling them "Harijans," which means "children of God."

The government has thrown its full weight behind the program of giving the Harijans an equal chance in society—especially when it comes to job opportunities, education and housing.

India's leaders, in and out of government, are conscious of their country's other great problems and are heroically grappling with them. The country seems to be divided. Some say that India should become westernized and modernized as quickly as possible so that she might raise her standards of living. Foreign capital and foreign industry should be invited in, for in this lies the salvation of the almost desperate situation.

On the other hand, there are others—perhaps the majority—who say that westernization will bring with it the evils of materialism, cut throat competition and rugged individualism; that India will lose her soul if she takes to chasing Yankee dollars; and that the big machine will only raise the living standards of the comparative few workers who get jobs but that the greater number of people will be displaced and will thus be worse off than they are now.

Prime Minister Nehru, who is at once an intellectual and a man charged with the practical responsibility of heading the government, seems to steer a middle course between these extreme attitudes. In our talk with him he indicated that he felt that some industrialization was absolutely necessary; that there were some things that only big or heavy industry could do for the country but that if the state keeps a watchful eye on the developments, most of the pitfalls may be avoided.

At the same time, Mr. Nehru gives support to the movement that would encourage and expand the handicraft arts such as spinning and weaving in home and village and thus leaving as much economic self help and autonomy as possible to the local community.

There is a great movement in India that is almost unknown in America. At its center is the campaign for land reform known as Bhoodan. It would solve India's great economic and social change by consent, not by force. The Bhoodanists are led by the sainted Vinoba Bhave and Jayaprakash Narayan, a highly sensitive intellectual who was trained in American colleges. Their ideal is the self-sufficient village. Their program envisions

1. *Persuading* large land owners to give up some of their holding to landless peasants;

2. *Persuading* small land owners to give up their individual ownership for common cooperative ownership by the villages;

3. *Encouraging* farmers and villagers to spin and weave the cloth for their own clothes during their spare time from their agricultural pursuits.

Since these measures would answer the questions of employment, food and clothing, the village could then, through cooperative action, make just about everything that it would need or get it through barter or exchange from other villages. Accordingly, each village would be virtually self sufficient and would thus free itself from the domination of the urban centers that are today like evil lodestones drawing the people away from the rural areas, concentrating them in city slums and debauching them with urban vices. At least this is the argument of the Bhoodanists and other Gandhians.

Such ideas sound strange and archaic to Western ears. However, the Indians have already achieved greater results than we Americans would ever expect. For example, millions of acres of land have been given up by rich landlords and additional millions of acres have been given up to cooperative management by small farmers. On the other hand, the Bhoodanists shrink from giving their movement the organization and drive that we in America would venture to guess that it must have in order to keep pace with the magnitude of the problems that everybody is trying to solve.

Even the government's five-year plans fall short in that they do not appear to be of sufficient scope to embrace their objectives. Thus, the three five-year plans were designed to provide 25,000,000 new jobs over a 15 year period but the birth rate of India is 6,000,000 per year. This means that in 15 years there will be 9,000,000 more people (less those who have died or retired) looking for the 15 million new jobs. In other words, if the planning were 100 per cent successful, it could not keep pace with the growth of problems it is trying to solve.

As for what should be done, we surely do not have the answer. But we do feel certain that India needs help. She must have outside capital and technical know-how. It is in the interest of the United States and the West to help supply these needs and *not attach strings to the gifts.*

Whatever we do should be done in a spirit of international brotherhood, not national selfishness. It should be done not merely because it is diplomatically expedient, but because it is morally compelling. At the same time, it will rebound to the credit of the West if India is able to maintain her democracy while solving her problems.

It would be a boon to democracy if one of the great nations of the world, with almost 400,000,000 people, proves that it is possible to provide a good living for everyone without surrendering to a dictatorship of either the "right" or "left." Today India is a tremendous force for peace and non-violence, at home and abroad. It is a land where the idealist and the intellectual are yet respected. We should want to help India preserve her soul and thus help to save our own.

"Jawaharlal Nehru, a Leader in the Long Anti-Colonial Struggle"

Article by Martin Luther King, Jr.

From *Legacy of Nehru*

ATLANTA, GEORGIA, FEBRUARY 8, 1965

———◇◇◇———

Jawaharlal Nehru was a man of three extraordinary epochs. He was a leader in the long anti-colonial struggle to free his own land and to inspire a fighting will in other lands under bondage.

He lived to see victory and to move then to another epochal confrontation—the fight for peace after World War II. In this climactic struggle he did not have Gandhi at his side, but he did have the Indian people now free in their own great Republic.

It would be hard to overstate Nehru's and India's contributions in this period. It was a time fraught with the constant threat of a devastating finality for mankind. There was no moment in this period free from the peril of atomic war. In these years Nehru was a towering world force skillfully inserting the peace will of India between the raging antagonisms of the great powers of East and West.

The world needed a mediator and an "honest broker" lest, in its sudden acquisition of overwhelming destructive force, one side or the other might plunge the world into mankind's last war. Nehru had the prestige, the wisdom, and the daring to play the role.

The markedly relaxed tensions of to-day are Nehru's legacy to us and at the same time they are our monument to him.

It should not be forgotten that the treaty to end nuclear testing accomplished 1963 was first proposed by Nehru. Let us also remember that the world dissolution of colonialism now speedily unfolding had its essential origins in India's massive victory. And let it also be remembered that Nehru guided into being the "Asian-African Bloc" as a united voice for the billions who were groping toward a modern world. He was the architect of the policy of non-alignment or neutralism which was calculated to give independent expression to the emerging nations while enabling them to play a constructive role in world affairs.

The third epoch of Nehru's work is unfolding after his death. Even though his physical presence is gone his spiritual influence retains a living force. The great powers are not yet in harmonious relationships to each other, but with the help of the non-aligned world they have learned to exercise a wise restraint. In this is the basis for a lasting detente. Beyond this, Nehru's example in daring to believe and act for peaceful co-existence gives mankind its most glowing hope.

In this period my people, the Negroes of the United States have made strides toward freedom beyond all precedent in our history. Our successes directly derive from our employment of the tactics of non-violent direct action and non-cooperation with evil which Nehru effectively employed under Gandhi's inspiration.

The peculiar genius of Imperialism was found in its capacity to delude so much of the world into the belief that it was civilizing primitive cultures even though it was grossly exploiting them.

Satyagraha made the myth transparent as it revealed the oppressed to be the truly civilized party. They rejected violence but maintained resistance, while the oppressor knew nothing but the use of violence.

My people found that Satyagraha applied in the U.S. to our oppressors also clarified who was right and who was wrong. On this foundation of truth an irresistible majority could be organized for just solutions.

Our fight is not yet won, just as the struggle against colonialism is still unfinished, and above all, the achievement of a stable peace still lies ahead of, and not behind us.

In all of these struggles of mankind to rise to a true state of civilization, the towering figure of Nehru sits unseen but felt at all council tables. He is missed by the world, and because he is so wanted, he is a living force in the tremulous world of today.

PART IV

For the Least of These:
Launching the Global War on Poverty

*The maintenance of peace requires the promotion of
justice, and for almost seventy-five per cent of the world's
population, justice requires development. When progress
and development are neglected, conflict is inevitable.
We of the West must come to see that the so-called wars of
liberation which loom on the world horizon are attempts
of the people of under-developed nations to find freedom
from hunger, disease and exploitation. They need not en-
tail the overthrow of governments if these governments
are sensitive, non-oppressive, and non-corrupt.*

— A statement at Pacem In Terris II Convocation,
Geneva, Switzerland, May 29, 1967

Introduction

The magnitude of the problem of poverty worldwide was astonishing and difficult to assess in Martin Luther King, Jr.'s time. In rich and poor countries around the globe, millions suffered immensely due to the scarcity and lack of food, clean and fresh drinking water, clothing and shelter, health care, and education. King persistently addressed these problems in his sermons, speeches, and writings, and he also led campaigns that attacked poverty and joblessness while offering constructive proposals for effective action to meet basic human needs through governmental and private initiatives. King hoped that his assault on poor housing and unjust real estate practices in Chicago in 1965 and '66, his planned Poor People's Campaign in the United States in 1967 and '68, and his involvement in the Memphis Sanitation Strike in early 1968 would serve as models for constructive action against poverty in America and abroad.

King's three statements in part IV of this volume are among his most profound reflections on world poverty and on the need for new global economic strategies to serve the best interests of what he called "the least of these." King spoke clearly and compellingly to a nation and a world that often seemed oblivious to the suffering of "these poverty-stricken children of God," reminding them that the interests of the poor and destitute should never be reduced to secondary importance. Convinced that space and resources should never be limited to certain people at the expense of others, King attacked the structural factors that caused and perpetuated poverty, and urged the people of the world to become more environmentally conscious and responsible, to unite in protecting the earth and its resources, to be prepared to sacrifice for the common good, and to take the necessary steps to insure universal prosperity and human welfare.

King's statement "The Octopus of Poverty" is the first to appear in part IV. Published in a periodical called the *Mennonite*, on January 5, 1965, this statement highlights the evils of global poverty, noting particularly "the social and economic gulf" that separated "the haves" from "the have nots of the world." King closed with a stern reminder to the rich regarding their moral responsibility to the poor, a concern he framed in biblical terms in his sermons on the rich young ruler (Matthew 19:16–23), the Good Samaritan (Luke 10:29–37), and "Lazarus and Divas" (Luke 16:19–31). Here King actually reframed the terms of the debate around poverty, especially in a culture in which the poor were too often blamed for their own condition.

The second statement, "Poverty and the World House," is included because it underscores, perhaps more than any other King document, the enormous threat that poverty poses for the global community. The point here is that "the world house," or the global beloved community, can never be actualized as long as millions across the world languish in grinding poverty. In this statement, King brings not only poor people but poor nations into the sphere of his moral vision. He called for cooperative international ventures on the part of wealthy nations that would benefit undeveloped and underdeveloped nations, particularly in terms of capital and technical assistance. At the same time, King was always mindful of how heads of state and dictators in poor countries routinely exploited their subjects while pursuing notoriously lavish lifestyles. For King, this was all too evident in parts of Africa, Asia, Latin America, and the Caribbean, leading in some cases to popular uprisings, and he addressed the issue at times with the penetrating insight of a social scientist and the boldness and uncompromising spirit of a prophet.

The final statement in part IV, "Nonviolence and Social Change," is included here because it expresses King's sense of the relationship between poverty and violence. In King's estimation, global poverty really amounted to massive violence against the human family. The deprivation and depression caused by poverty worldwide were, as King determined, clear evidence of pervasive psychological violence—and even physical violence as well. Such a perspective came only naturally for King, who abhorred violence in all of its painful expressions and who consistently raised the need for universal standards of common decency that gave top priority to human welfare and survival.

Also in "Nonviolence and Social Change," King established the connection between poverty in America and poverty in other parts of the world. His focus on the interrelated structures of poverty at home and abroad reveals the profundity of his insight into the nature of social evil in his time. Moreover, King never separated his own campaigns on behalf of the poor in the United States from the struggles of the poor in Africa, Asia, Latin America, and the Caribbean. For King, the universe was made this way. He termed this "the interrelated structure of all reality," a principle he frequently gave expression to in his sermons, mass-meeting speeches, writings, and interviews.

Global poverty is perhaps as widespread today as it was in King's time. The current global economic crisis has led to rising food prices and cutbacks on aid to poor families and the elderly in the United States, and to occasional food crises, starvation, and death in poor countries in Africa, Asia, and the Caribbean. Homelessness is characteristic of life for millions in the so-called Third World, and it has reached epidemic proportions even in rich nations like the United States and Canada, a problem exacerbated by the population explosion. The rich are getting richer and the poor poorer, and few who live in luxury and security are willing to embrace and practice King's altruistic ethic, which affirms an unselfish and unwavering devotion to the uplift and empowerment of others.

As the documents in part IV of "In a Single Garment of Destiny" suggest, King still has much to say to the world about the evils of poverty and neglect, and about the wisdom of meeting basic human needs as an avenue to world community and peace. King reminded us that we discover our most authentic selves when we identify and walk with those in deepest need. His call for "coalitions of conscience" to address the problems of the poor, the weak, and the disabled is as urgent today as it was a half century ago, and so is his advocacy for more enlightened global economic policies. Caring for and serving the poverty-stricken and needy are not only consistent with King's legacy of ideas and struggle but also indicative of how human rights can still be universalized in principle and practice in this twenty-first-century world.

"The Octopus of Poverty"

Statement by Martin Luther King, Jr.

The Mennonite

JANUARY 5, 1965

—◇◇—

A second evil which plagues the modern world is that of poverty. Like a monstrous octopus, it projects its nagging, prehensile tentacles in lands and villages all over the world. The misery of the poor in Africa and Asia is shared misery, a fact of life for the vast majority, they are all poor together as a result of years in exploitation and underdevelopment. In sad contrast, the poor in America know that they live in the richest nation in the world, and that even though they are perishing on a lonely island of poverty they are surrounded by a vast ocean of material prosperity.

So it is obvious that if man is to redeem his spiritual and moral "lag" he must go all out to bridge the social and economic gulf between the *haves* and the *have nots* of the world. Poverty is one of the most urgent items on the agenda of modern life.

There is nothing new about poverty. What is new, however, is that we have the resources to get rid of it.

The time has come for an all-out war against poverty. The rich nations must use their vast resources of wealth to develop the underdeveloped, school the unschooled, and feed the unfed. Ultimately a great nation is a compassionate nation. No individual or nation can be great if it does not have a concern for *the least of these.*

In the final analysis, the rich must not ignore the poor because both rich and poor are tied in a single garment of destiny. All life is interrelated, and all men are interdependent. The agony of the poor diminishes the rich, and the salvation of the poor enlarges the rich. We are inevitably our brother's keeper because of the interrelated structure of reality.

LOVE PEACE AND SACRIFICE FOR IT

A third great evil confronting our world is that of war. The fact that most of the time human beings put the truth about the nature and risks of the nuclear war out of their minds because it is too painful and therefore not "acceptable," does not alter the nature and risks of such war.

But wisdom born of experience should tell us that war is obsolete. If we assume that life is worth living and that man has a right to survive, then we must find an alternative to war.

Therefore, I venture to suggest that the philosophy and strategy of nonviolence become immediately a subject for study and for serious experimentation in every field of human conflict, by no means excluding the relations between nations.

I do not wish to minimize the complexity of the problems that need to be faced in achieving disarmament and peace. But I think it is a fact that we shall not have the will, the courage and the insight to deal with such matters unless in this field we are prepared to undergo a mental and spiritual re-evaluation—a change of focus which will enable us to see that the things which seem most real and powerful are indeed now unreal and have come under the sentence of death.

We will not build a peaceful world by following a negative path. It is not enough to say "We must not wage war." It is necessary to love peace and sacrifice for it.

So we must fix our visions not merely on the negative expulsion of war, but upon the positive affirmation of peace. In short, we just shift the arms into a *peace race*.

"Poverty and the World House"

Statement by Martin Luther King, Jr.

From *Where Do We Go from Here:
Chaos or Community?*

1967

Another grave problem that must be solved if we are to live creatively in our world house is that of poverty on an international scale. Like a monstrous octopus, it stretches its choking, prehensile tentacles into lands and villages all over the world. Two-thirds of the peoples of the world go to bed hungry at night. They are undernourished, ill-housed and shabbily clad. Many of them have no houses or beds to sleep in. Their only beds are the sidewalks of the cities and the dusty roads of the villages. Most of these poverty-stricken children of God have never seen a physician or a dentist.

There is nothing new about poverty. What is new, however, is that we now have the resources to get rid of it. Not too many years ago, Dr. Kirtley Mather, a Harvard geologist, wrote a book entitled *Enough and to Spare*. He set forth the basic theme that famine is wholly unnecessary in the modern world. Today, therefore, the question on the agenda must read: why should there be hunger and privation in any land, in any city, at any table, when man has the resources and the scientific know-how to provide all mankind with the basic necessities of life? Even deserts can be irrigated and topsoil can be replaced. We cannot complain of a lack of land, for there are 25 million square miles of tillable land on earth, of which we are using less than seven million. We have amazing knowledge of vitamins, nutrition, the chemistry of food and the versatility of atoms. There is no deficit in human resources; the deficit is in human will.

This does not mean that we can overlook the enormous acceleration in the rate of growth of the world's population. The population explosion is very real, and it must be faced squarely if we are to avoid, in centuries ahead, a "standing room only" situation on these earthly shores. Most of the large undeveloped nations in the world today are confronted with the problem of excess population in relation to resources. But even this problem will be greatly diminished by wiping out poverty. When people see more opportunities for better education and greater economic security, they begin to consider whether a smaller family might not be better for themselves and for their children. In other words, I doubt that there can be a stabilization of the population without a prior stabilization of economic resources.

The time has come for an all-out world war against poverty. The rich nations must use their vast resources of wealth to develop the underdeveloped, school the unschooled and feed the unfed. The well-off and the secure have too often become indifferent and oblivious to the poverty and deprivation in their midst. The poor in our countries have been shut out of our minds, and driven from the mainstream of our societies, because we have allowed them to become invisible. Ultimately a great nation is a compassionate nation. No individual or nation can be great if it does not have a concern for "the least of these."

The first step in the worldwide war against poverty is passionate commitment. All the wealthy nations—America, Britain, Russia, Canada, Australia, and those of Western Europe—must see it as a moral obligation to provide capital and technical assistance to the underdeveloped areas. These rich nations have only scratched the surface in their commitment. There is need now for a general strategy of support. Sketchy aid here and there will not suffice, nor will it sustain economic growth. There must be a sustained effort extending through many years. The wealthy nations of the world must promptly initiate a massive, sustained Marshall Plan for Asia, Africa and South America. If they would allocate just 2 percent of their gross national product annually for a period of ten or twenty years for the development of the underdeveloped nations, mankind would go a long way toward conquering the ancient enemy, poverty.

The aid program that I am suggesting must not be used by the wealthy nations as a surreptitious means to control the poor nations. Such an approach would lead to a new form of paternalism and a neocolonialism which no self-respecting nation could accept. Ultimately, foreign aid programs must be motivated by a compassionate and committed effort to wipe poverty, ignorance and disease from the face of the earth. Money devoid of genuine empathy is like salt devoid of savor, good for nothing except to be trodden under foot of men.

The West must enter into the program with humility and penitence and a sober realization that everything will not always "go our way." It cannot be forgotten that the Western powers were but yesterday the colonial masters. The house of the West is far from in order, and its hands are far from clean.

We must have patience. We must be willing to understand why many of the young nations will have to pass through the same extremism, revolution and aggression that formed our own history. Every new government confronts overwhelming problems. During the days when they were struggling to remove the yoke of colonialism, there was a kind of preexistent unity of purpose that kept things moving in one solid direction. But as soon as independence emerges, all the grim problems of life confront them with stark realism: the lack of capital, the strangulating poverty, the uncontrollable birth rates and, above all, the high aspirational level of their own people. The postcolonial period is more difficult and precarious than the colonial struggle itself.

The West must also understand that its economic growth took place under rather propitious circumstances. Most of the Western nations were relatively underpopulated when they surged forward economically, and they were greatly endowed with the iron ore and coal that were needed for launching industry. Most of the young governments of the world today have come into being without these advantages, and, above all, they confront staggering problems of overpopulation. There is no possible way for them to make it without aid and assistance.

A genuine program on the part of the wealthy nations to make prosperity a reality for the poor nations will in the final analysis enlarge the prosperity of all. One of the best proofs that reality hinges on moral foundations is the fact that when men and governments work devotedly for the good of others, they achieve their own enrichment in the process.

From time immemorial men have lived by the principle that "self-preservation is the first law of life." But this is a false assumption. I would say that other-preservation is the first law of life. It is the first law of life precisely because we cannot preserve self without being concerned about preserving other selves. The universe is so structured that things go awry if men are not diligent in their cultivation of the other regarding dimension. "I" cannot reach fulfillment without "thou." The self cannot be self without other selves. Self-concern without other-concern is like a tributary that has no outward flow to the ocean. Stagnant, still and stale, it lacks both life and freshness. Nothing would be more disastrous and out of harmony with our self-interest than for the developed nations to travel a dead-end road of inordinate selfishness. We are in the fortunate position of having our deepest sense of morality coalesce with our self-interest.

But the real reason that we must use our resources to outlaw poverty goes beyond material concerns to the quality of our mind and spirit. Deeply woven into the fiber of our religious tradition is the conviction that men are made in the image of God, and that they are souls of infinite metaphysical value. If we accept this as a profound moral fact, we cannot be content to see men hungry, to see men victimized with ill-health, when we have the means to help them. In the final analysis, the rich must not ignore the poor because both rich and poor are tied together. They entered the same mysterious gateway of human birth, into the same adventure of mortal life.

All men are interdependent. Every nation is an heir of a vast treasury of ideas and labor to which both the living and the dead of all nations have contributed. Whether we realize it or not, each of us lives eternally "in the red." We are everlasting debtors to known and unknown men and women. When we arise in the morning, we go into the bathroom where we reach for a sponge which is provided for us by a Pacific Islander. We reach for soap that is created for us by a European. Then at the table we drink coffee which is provided for us by a South American, or tea by a Chinese or cocoa by a West African. Before we leave for our jobs we are already beholden to more than half of the world.

In a real sense, all life is interrelated. The agony of the poor impoverishes the rich; the betterment of the poor enriches the rich. We are inevitably our brother's keeper because we are our brother's brother. Whatever affects one directly affects all indirectly.

"Nonviolence and Social Change"

Statement by Martin Luther King, Jr.

From *The Trumpet of Conscience*

1968

There is nothing wrong with a traffic law which says you have to stop for a red light. But when a fire is raging, the fire truck goes right through that red light, and normal traffic had better get out of its way. Or, when a man is bleeding to death, the ambulance goes through those red lights at top speed.

There is a fire raging now for the Negroes and the poor of this society. They are living in tragic conditions because of the terrible economic injustices that keep them locked in as an "underclass," as the sociologists are now calling it. Disinherited people all over the world are bleeding to death from deep social and economic wounds. They need brigades of ambulance drivers who will have to ignore the red lights of the present system until the emergency is solved.

Massive civil disobedience is a strategy for social change which is at least as forceful as an ambulance with its siren on full. In the past ten years, nonviolent civil disobedience has made a great deal of history, especially in the Southern United States. When we and the Southern Christian Leadership Conference went to Birmingham, Alabama, in 1963, we had decided to take action on the matter of integrated public accommodations. We went knowing that the Civil Rights Commission had written powerful documents calling for change, calling for the very rights we were demanding. But nobody did anything about the Commission's report. Nothing was done until we acted on these very issues, and demonstrated before the court of world opinion the urgent need for change. It was the same story with voting rights. The Civil Rights Commission, three years before we went to Selma, had recommended the changes we started marching for, but nothing was done until, in 1965, we created a crisis the nation couldn't ignore. Without violence, we totally disrupted the system, the lifestyle of Birmingham, and then of Selma, with their unjust and unconstitutional laws. Our Birmingham struggle came to its dramatic climax when some 3,500 demonstrators virtually filled every jail in that city and surrounding communities, and some 4,000 more continued to march and demonstrate nonviolently. The city knew then in terms that were crystal clear that Birmingham could no longer continue to function until the demands of the Negro community were met. The same kind of dramatic crisis was created in Selma two years later. The result on the national scene was the Civil Rights Bill and the Voting Rights Act, as President and Congress responded to the drama and the creative tension generated by the carefully planned demonstrations.

Of course, by now it is obvious that new laws are not enough. The emergency we now face is economic, and it is a desperate and worsening situation. For the 35 million poor people in America— not even to mention, just yet, the poor in the other nations—there is a kind of strangulation in the air. In our society it is murder, psychologically, to deprive a man of a job or an income. You are in substance saying to that man that he has no right to exist. You are in a real way depriving him of life, liberty, and the pursuit of happiness, denying in his case the very creed of his society. Now, millions of people are being strangled that way. The problem is international in scope. And it is getting worse, as the gap between the poor and the "affluent society" increases.

The question that now divides the people who want radically to change that situation is: can a program of nonviolence—even if it envisions massive civil disobedience—realistically expect to deal with such an enormous, entrenched evil?

First of all, will nonviolence work, psychologically, after the summer of 1967? Many people feel that nonviolence as a strategy for social change was cremated in the flames of the urban riots of the last two years. They tell us that Negroes have only now begun to find their true manhood in violence; that the riots prove not only that Negroes hate whites, but that, compulsively, they must destroy them.

This bloodlust interpretation ignores one of the most striking features of the city riots. Violent they certainly were. But the violence, to a startling degree, was focused against property rather than against people. There were very few cases of injury to persons, and the vast majority of the rioters were not involved at all in attacking people. The much publicized "death toll" that marked the riots, and the many injuries, were overwhelmingly inflicted on the rioters by the military. It is clear that the riots were exacerbated by police action that was designed to injure or even to kill people. As for the snipers, no account of the riots claims that more than one or two dozen people were involved in sniping. From the facts, an unmistakable pattern emerges: a handful of Negroes used gunfire substantially to intimidate, not to kill; and all of the other participants had a different target—property.

I am aware that there are many who wince at a distinction between property and persons—who hold both sacrosanct. My views are not so rigid. A life is sacred. Property is intended to serve life, and no matter how much we surround it with rights and respect, it has no personal being. It is part of the earth man walks on; it is not man.

The focus on property in the 1967 riots is not accidental. It has a message; it is saying something.

If hostility to whites were ever going to dominate a Negro's attitude and reach murderous proportions, surely it would be during a riot. But this rare opportunity for bloodletting was sublimated into arson, or turned into a kind of stormy carnival of free-merchandise distribution. Why did the rioters avoid personal attacks? The explanation cannot be fear of retribution, because the physical risks incurred in the attacks on property were no less than for personal assaults. The military forces were treating acts of petty larceny as equal to murder. Far more rioters took chances with their own lives, in their attacks on property, than threatened the life of anyone else. Why were they so violent with property then? Because property represents the white power structure, which they were attacking and trying to destroy. A curious proof of the symbolic aspect of the looting for some who took part in it is the fact that, after the riots, police received hundreds of calls from Negroes trying to return merchandise they had taken. Those people wanted the experience of taking, of redressing the power imbalance that property represents. Possession, afterward, was secondary.

A deeper level of hostility came out in arson, which was far more dangerous than the looting. But it, too, was a demonstration and a warning. It was directed against symbols of exploitation, and it was designed to express the depth of anger in the community.

What does this restraint in the summer riots mean for our future strategy?

If one can find a core of nonviolence toward persons, even during the riots when emotions were exploding, it means that nonviolence should not be written off for the future as a force in Negro life. Many people believe that the urban Negro is too angry and too sophisticated to be nonviolent. Those same people dismiss the nonviolent marches in the South and try to describe them as processions of pious, elderly ladies. The fact is that in all the marches we have organized some men of very violent tendencies have been involved. It was routine for us to collect hundreds of knives from our own ranks before the demonstrations, in case of momentary weakness. And in Chicago last year we saw some of the most violent individuals accepting nonviolent discipline. Day after day during those Chicago marches I walked in our lines and I never saw anyone retaliate with violence. There were lots of provocations, not only the screaming white hoodlums lining the sidewalks, but also groups of Negro militants talking about guerrilla warfare. We had some gang leaders and members marching with us. I remember walking with the Blackstone Rangers while bottles were flying from the sidelines, and I saw their noses being broken and blood flowing from their wounds; and I saw them continue and not retaliate, not one of them, with violence. I am convinced that even very violent temperaments can be channeled through nonviolent discipline, if the movement is moving, if they can act constructively and express through an effective channel their very legitimate anger.

But even if nonviolence can be valid, psychologically, for the protesters who want change, is it going to be effective, strategically, against a government and a status quo that have so far resisted this summer's demands on the grounds that "we must not reward the rioters"? Far from rewarding the rioters, far from even giving a hearing to their just and urgent demands, the administration has ignored its responsibility for the causes of the riots, and instead has used the negative aspects of them to justify continued inaction on the underlying issues. The administration's only concrete response was to initiate a study and call for a day of prayer. As a minister, I take prayer too seriously to use it as an excuse for avoiding work and responsibility. When a government commands more wealth and power than has ever been known in the history of the world, and offers no more than this, it is worse than blind, it is provocative. It is paradoxical but fair to say that Negro terrorism is incited less on ghetto street corners than in the halls of Congress.

I intended to show that nonviolence will be effective, but not until it has achieved the massive dimensions, the disciplined planning, and the intense commitment of a sustained, direct-action movement of civil disobedience on the national scale.

The dispossessed of this nation—the poor, both white and Negro—live in a cruelly unjust society. They must organize a revolution against that injustice, not against the lives of the persons who are their fellow citizens, but against the structures through which the society is refusing to take means which have been called for, and which are at hand, to lift the load of poverty.

The only real revolutionary, people say, is a man who has nothing to lose. There are millions of poor people in this country who have very little, or even nothing, to lose. If they can be helped to take action together, they will do so with a freedom and a power that will be a new and unsettling force in our complacent national life. Beginning in the New Year, we will be recruiting three thousand of the poorest citizens from ten different urban and rural areas to initiate and lead a sustained, massive, direct-action movement in Washington. Those who choose to join this initial three thousand, this nonviolent army, this "freedom church" of the poor, will work with us for three months to develop nonviolent action skills. Then we will move on Washington, determined to stay there until the legislative and executive branches of the government take serious and adequate action on jobs and income. A delegation of poor people can walk into a high official's office with a carefully, collectively prepared list of demands. (If you're poor, if you're unemployed anyway, you can choose to stay in Washington as long as the struggle needs you.) And if that official says, "But Congress would have to approve this," or, "But the President would have to be consulted on that," you can say, "All right, we'll wait." And you can settle down in his office for as long a stay as necessary. If you are, let's say, from rural Mississippi, and have never had medical attention, and your children are undernourished and unhealthy, you can take those little children into the Washington hospitals and stay with them there until the medical workers cope with their needs, and in showing it your children you will have shown this country a sight that will make it stop in its busy tracks and think hard about what it has done. The many people who will come and join this three thousand, from all groups in the country's life, will play a supportive role, deciding to be poor for a time along with the dispossessed who are asking for their right to jobs or income—jobs, income, the demolition of slums, and the rebuilding by the people who live there of new communities in their place; in fact, a new economic deal for the poor.

Why camp in Washington to demand these things? Because only the federal Congress and administration can decide to use the billions of dollars we need for a real war on poverty. We need, not a new law, but a massive, new national program. This Congress has done nothing to help such measures, and plenty to hinder them. Why should Congress care about our dying cities? It is still dominated by senior representatives of the rural South, who still unite in an obstructive coalition with unprogressive Northerners to prevent public funds from going where they are socially needed. We broke that coalition in 1963 and 1964, when the Civil Rights and Voting Rights laws were passed. We need to break it again by the size and force of our movement, and the best place to do that is before the eyes and inside the buildings of these same Congressmen. The people of this country, if not the Congressmen, are ready for a serious economic attack on slums and unemployment, as two recent polls by Lou Harris have revealed. So we have to make Congress ready to act on the plight of the poor. We will prod and sensitize the legislators, the administrators, and all the wielders of power until they have faced this utterly imperative need.

I have said that the problem, the crisis we face, is international in scope. In fact, it is inseparable from an international emergency which involves the poor, the dispossessed, and the exploited of the whole world.

Can a nonviolent, direct-action movement find application on the international level, to confront economic and political problems? I believe it can. It is clear to me that the next stage of the movement is to become international. National movements within the developed countries—forces that focus on London, or Paris, or Washington, or Ottawa—must help to make it politically feasible for their governments to undertake the kind of massive aid that the developing countries need if they are to break the chains of poverty. We in the West must bear in mind that the poor countries are poor primarily because we have exploited them through political or economic colonialism. Americans in particular must help their nation repent of her modern economic imperialism.

But movements in our countries alone will not be enough. In Latin America, for example, national reform movements have almost despaired of nonviolent methods; many young men, even many priests, have joined guerrilla movements in the hills. So many of Latin America's problems have roots in the United States of America that we need to form a solid, united movement, nonviolently conceived and carried through, so that pressure can be brought to bear on the capital and government power structures concerned, from both sides of the problem at once. I think that may be the only hope for a nonviolent solution in Latin America today; and one of the most powerful expressions of nonviolence may come out of that international coalition of socially aware forces, operating outside governmental frameworks.

Even entrenched problems like the South African Government and its racial policies could be tackled on this level. If just two countries, Britain and the United States, could be persuaded to end all economic interaction with the South African regime, they could bring that government to its knees in a relatively short time. Theoretically, the British and American governments could make that kind of decision; almost every corporation in both countries has economic ties with its government which it could not afford to do without. In practice, such a decision would represent such a major reordering of priorities that we should not expect that any movement could bring it about in one year or two. Indeed, although it is obvious that nonviolent movements for social change must internationalize, because of the interlocking nature of the problems they all face, and because otherwise those problems will breed war, we have hardly begun to build the skills and the strategy, or even the commitment, to planetize our movement for social justice.

In a world facing the revolt of ragged and hungry masses of God's children; in a world torn between the tensions of East and West, white and colored, individualists and collectivists; in a world whose cultural and spiritual power lags so far behind her technological capabilities that we live each day on the verge of nuclear co-annihilation; in this world, nonviolence is no longer an option for intellectual analysis, it is an imperative for action.

PART V

To Study War No More:
An Affirmation of World Peace
and Human Coexistence

The civilized world stands on the brink of nuclear annihilation. No longer can any sensible person talk glibly about preparation for war. The present crisis calls for sober thinking, reasonable negotiation and moral commitment. More than ever before the Gandhian method of nonviolent direct action must be applied in international affairs. This method must not be seen as merely a method to be used in conflicts within nations. It must be seen as a method which can be creatively used to resolve conflicts among the power blocks in the world today. Moreover, it must be used to arouse the conscience of these nations on the whole question of disarmament.

— A letter to Mr. G. Ramachandran, editor of *Gandhi Marg*, Rajghat, New Delhi, India, December 20, 1961

Introduction

D r. King went through a kind of spiritual and intellectual odyssey on the whole question of war. Prior to his emergence as a civil rights leader, he thought that war could serve as "a necessary evil" or "negative good," which means, more specifically, that it could be waged to end the rise of an evil force in history like an Adolf Hitler. After receiving the Nobel Peace Prize in 1964, King consistently declared that weapons of mass destruction rendered war "obsolete"; that the destructive power of atomic and nuclear weapons "eliminated even the possibility that war could serve any good at all." Convinced that violence in any form is intrinsically immoral and impractical, King was deeply concerned about the looming specter of war and its potential for global human catastrophe. Thus, he urged the United States and other powerful nations not only to stem the tide of nuclear proliferation and work toward disarmament but also to become global leaders in creating a world in which peace is an enduring goal and prosperity is universally shared.

Driven by the belief that war only breeds more war, King pursued world peace himself with an unrelenting passion. He proclaimed the gospel of peace in his sermons, speeches, and writings; marched with activists in the peace movement in the late 1960s; and called for global organizing and activism in the interest of peaceful coexistence between peoples of different nationalities. Even so, King never thought of himself in a grandiose way or as the one person given to peace who could cause the transformation of the whole world. To the contrary, his hope was that the different peoples of the world might be transformed into a community of peace-loving and peace-making nations. As far as King was concerned, humanity stood at a crossroads where the choice between "nonviolent coexistence" and "violent coannihilation" had never been clearer and more urgent.

The speeches and statements that comprise part V of "*In a*

Single Garment of Destiny" reveal the keen sense of urgency King brought to his analysis of the problem of war and its catastrophic consequences. King's "Address at the Thirty-sixth Annual Dinner of the War Resisters League" in New York in February 1959 is included here as one of King's earliest calls for the total eradication of war. In it, King also declared that the quest for social justice in the United States could not be separated from the enduring crusade for peace abroad. These two concerns conflated in his mind as he addressed both the timeless themes of war and peace and the purpose and value of human life and existence. To be sure, his most significant and far-reaching influence was perhaps his commitment to world peace.

Statements by King are included under the general topic "The Greatest Hope for World Peace." On November 5, 1964, King submitted these written statements as answers to a series of questions about war raised to him by *Redbook Magazine*. In these statements, King dealt with issues such as the futility of war, the role of the United Nations as a peace-making and peace-keeping force, the question of the justifiability of war, the steps that the average person could take in advancing world peace, and his own perspective on how a "permanent world peace" might be achieved. Clearly, King did not accept the rationale for using military force to try to remedy the world's problems. Unlike many Americans in his time, King also insisted that democratic freedoms should be spread by example rather than by military might. Peaceful ends, he frequently declared, could only be secured through peaceful means.

King's speech "The Casualties of the War in Vietnam," delivered at the Nation Institute in Los Angeles on February 25, 1967, also appears in complete form in part V. Here King used the Vietnam conflict to highlight the evils of war in general, but he was particularly concerned about what he called "the physical casualties" and "the casualties of principles and values" associated with the Vietnam War. He decried U.S. involvement in Vietnam, calling it, on numerous occasions, "a misadventure," and he concluded that the answer to the problems of the Vietnamese people rested with "the principle of self-determination," not with a militarized foreign policy. For King, the Vietnam War showed the sinister side of America, a nation for which even humanitarian intervention often served as a front for the invasion of weaker countries. Furthermore, he was convinced that America's military actions in so many instances were antiglobalist in nature.

The historic speech "Beyond Vietnam: A Time to Break Silence" was given at a meeting of Clergy and Laity Concerned (CALC) at the Riverside Church in New York City on April 4, 1967, exactly one year prior to King's assassination. This speech is provided here for essentially two reasons. First, because it was King's most compelling statement on the negative impact of the Vietnam War on the civil rights program in the United States and particularly its war on poverty. Second, in it King criticized the war policy of the Johnson administration with fervor and in terms he had never used before. Moreover, King gave voice to the devastating impact of the war on the Vietnamese people and their livelihood, and set forth a five-step plan for ending "the nightmarish conflict." By this time, King was exploring more radical forms of nonviolence and massive civil disobedience, and was even advocating conscientious objection to war as an act of conscience.

The statement by King and the Southern Christian Leadership Conference (SCLC), "The Middle East Question," is among the most interesting documents in part V in part because it speaks to the timelessness of certain concerns raised by King with respect to world peace. This statement, which was set forth at the Chicago Conference of New Politics in September 1967, expressed King's views on how the violent conflict between the Israelis and the Palestinians might best be resolved. Clearly, King and his associates were concerned not only about the security of the state of Israel and its right to exist but also about the "imposed" state of "poverty and backwardness" that afflicted the Palestinians and the Arab world as a whole. In King's judgment, the Israeli-Palestinian conflict was one of the greatest threats to global peace efforts.

King spoke at greater length concerning the Middle East crisis in a number of interviews, the contents of which are not included in part V. In an interview on *Issues and Answers* with ABC-TV's Atlanta bureau chief Tom Jarriel and Washington correspondent John Casserly in June 1967, King asserted that "any talk of driving the Jews into the Mediterranean, as we have heard over the last few weeks or the last several years, is not only unrealistic talk but it is suicidal talk for the whole world, and I think also it is terribly immoral." King went on to state that "peace in the Middle East" also meant "Arab development." "After all, the Arab world is that third world, a part of that third world of poverty and illiteracy and disease," he declared, "and it is time now to have a Marshall Plan for the Middle East." In the middle of the interview with Jarriel and Casserly, King expressed the hope that countries like the United States, the Soviet Union, France, and Britain would use their influence to press for a solution to the Middle East conflict through the UN. Interestingly enough, King's thoughts on the security of Israel and the uplift and empowerment of the Palestinians are still being echoed by world leaders today, including President Barack Obama.

"War and the World House," taken from King's 1967 book *Where Do We Go from Here: Chaos or Community?*, is the concluding piece in part V. Here King concludes that war threatened the true realization of "the world house," and he put forth what was essentially a global ethic of peaceful coexistence. King attacked the impulse toward war, maintained that all of the global challenges could be met by an emphasis on peace, and envisioned a time when the whole world would live in harmony. He had come to believe that humankind's only option was to globalize the *agape* love ethic through nonviolence, to replace "the arms race" with "a peace race," and to reject the culture of war in favor of a culture of dialogue, cooperation, and peace.

When it came to the question of war, King's vision of "the world house," or a global beloved community, seems to carry a certain unrealistic quality, especially in this age of sectarian warfare, organized torture and terrorism, post–Cold War ethnic cleansings, genocide, religiously based violence, political assassinations, and violence, repression, and reprisal in the Middle East. The question for those who honor King today is, Was he hopelessly idealistic in his dream of a world devoid of war, or was he merely an intriguing blend of the realist and the idealist?

During his lifetime as well as posthumously, King continues to generate a huge level of interest in and debate about issues of war and peace. In fact, he anticipated debates around the logic of war and the necessity for peace advocacy that still rage in this increasingly complex, globalized, post-9/11 world. These debates are not likely to cease when nations disavow the Geneva Accords and other longstanding international agreements relative to the control of nuclear, biological, and chemical weapons, and when political and religious leaders give a kind of moral sanction to war as if it is a holy crusade. Clearly, the dynamics of global conflict have changed since King's death almost a half century ago. The global war on terror is defining much of human existence, and America has lost its aura of invincibility in the international community. Also, there is an even greater need for healing prescriptions to help nations to work through their complex problems and to build healthier and more productive relationships. But dialogue with King, around the ethics of war and peace, can still afford lessons for the present-day context of human conflict. After all, here was a man whose life was a testament to the power of nonviolence, who paid the ultimate price, and who had a spiritually charged devotion to saving humanity from tragic self-destruction. King's last two books (*Where Do We Go from Here* and *The Trumpet of Conscience*, from 1968) remain exceptional resources for discussions around war, peace, reconciliation, and community, especially as the tide of anti-Americanism continues to rise around the world.

The documents in part V are essential reading for all who believe in world peace, and they are most useful for peace activists and even for intelligence and counter-terrorism professionals, as well as for those who contend that more democracy and increased markets are essential steps in overcoming conflict across the globe. King has something to say to the entire world.

"Address at the Thirty-sixth Annual Dinner of the War Resisters League"

Address by Martin Luther King, Jr.

NEW YORK, NEW YORK, FEBRUARY 2, 1959

———⟨⟩———

I bring warm greetings from the embattled South—from fifty thousand Negroes of Montgomery, Alabama, from the S.C.L.C., uniting Negro leadership in twelve southern states representing the millions of Americans not yet recipients of the rights guaranteed in their own Constitution. I also bring greetings from your friends, and my colleagues, who keep the heroic struggle going regardless of its cost to them personally. Your sympathy and support mean a great deal to the fearless men who live daily with terror, and resist it with nonviolent power and determination.

I would not want you to feel that the pressures which surround southern resistance leaders obscure the positive gains our harassed movement is making. This week marks a turning point in our struggle. The defeat of massive resistance in Virginia is the Gettysburg of today. Governor [J. Lindsay] Almond with his army of political forces has had his lines broken, and has tasted defeat. This is significant because their resistance was total, but met its match in the total and active resistance of our forces. It was not alone expressions of good will from white moderates which weakened their ranks. Nor alone was it the legal manipulations and the successful utilization of court orders.

In Virginia Negroes themselves took into their own hands through direct action, the mobilizing of public opinion. CORE, NAACP, ministers, and labor, organized and conducted a march on the State Capitol in Richmond on January 1. Earlier in October, the S.C.L.C. brought to Norfolk Negro leaders from all over the South for a two day conference on non-violence. Though I was scheduled to be the principal speaker my confinement in the hospital made this impossible, but your A.J. Muste took my place and deepened in his inimitable fashion the thinking of our leaders on non-violence. At the conclusion of this conference, over 4,000 of the Negro citizens of Norfolk jammed the City Auditorium: the first demonstration of such numbers in the city's history, thus dramatizing the dynamic involvement of the community in this struggle. The whole press of Virginia front-paged this event making it unmistakably clear that the Negro of Virginia was not waiting submissively or passively for his rights to be handed to him. I have repeatedly warned my people that victory would not come if they wait for the white people to furnish the dinner while they merely furnish the appetite. The significant victory in Virginia illustrates that this lesson was learned and the fruits of active struggle, as always, is victory.

Not only in the South, but throughout the nation and the world, we live in an age of conflict, an age of biological weapons, chemical warfare, atomic fallout and nuclear bombs. It is a period of conflict between the mammoth powers. It is an age of conformity. It is a period of uncertainty and fear. Every man, woman and child lives, not knowing if they shall see tomorrow's sunrise.

We are in a period when men who understand the dimensions of our tragic state must be heard. We must stand up and accept the consequences of our convictions. First of all, we must resist war. With all our energy we must find our alternative to violence as a means to deal with the terrible conflicts that beset us.

We must no longer cooperate with policies that degrade man and make for war. The great need in the world today is to find the means for the social organization of the power of nonviolence.

In this connection, I salute the War Resisters League, which for thirty-six years has courageously carried on the fight against war. I applaud its members, many of whom chose prison rather than break their faith in the power of love. Some chose to be ostracized rather than engage in the brutalization of their fellow man.

You have been prophetic and, as Albert Einstein once said,

"You are part of the moral elite that may yet lead mankind from self-destruction."

As you know, the establishment of social justice in our nation is of profound concern to me. This great struggle is in the interest of all Americans and I shall not be turned from it. Yet no sane person can afford to work for social justice within the nation unless he simultaneously resists war and clearly declares himself for non-violence in international relations.

What will be the ultimate value of having established social justice in a context where all people, Negro and White, are merely free to face destruction by strontium 90 or atomic war?

If we are to find a new method to avoid such terrible possibilities, it will be based on love not hate; it will be based on reconciliation and not retaliation; it will be based on forgiveness and not on revenge.

If we are to find an alternative to war, we must re-examine the assumptions of the pacifist position.

My study of Gandhi convinced me that true pacifism is not nonresistance to evil; but nonviolent resistance to evil. Between the two positions, there is a world of difference. Gandhi resisted evil with as much vigor and power as the violent resister, but he resisted with love instead of hate. True pacifism is not unrealistic submission to evil power. . . . It is rather a courageous confrontation of evil by the power of love, in the faith that it is better to be the recipient of violence than the inflicter of it, since the latter only multiples the existence of violence and bitterness in the universe, while the former may develop a sense of shame in the opponent, and thereby bring about a transformation and change of heart. However bringing about such a transformation is not a simple matter. It requires directness of purpose, dedication and above all humility of mind and spirit. Because our thinking is so close, and because the task before us is so great, I feel free to say that we who believe in nonviolence often have an unwarranted optimism concerning man and lean unconsciously toward self-righteousness. It seems to me that we must see the pacifist position not as sinless but as the lesser evil in the circumstances. I have often felt that we who advocate nonviolence would have a greater appeal if we did not claim to be free from the moral dilemmas that the nonpacifist confronts.

Despite all shortcomings, the philosophy of nonviolence played such a positive role in the southern struggle that it may be wise to turn to a brief discussion of some basic aspects of nonviolence as they apply to Montgomery and may be applied to the quest for peace. First it must be emphasized that nonviolent resistance is not a method for cowards; it does resist. If one uses this method because he is afraid or merely because he lacks the instruments of violence, he is not truly nonviolent. This is why Gandhi often said that if cowardice is the only alternative to violence, it is better to fight. He made this statement conscious of the fact that there is always another alternative: no individual or group need submit to any wrong, nor need they use violence to right the wrong; there is the way of nonviolent resistance. This is ultimately the way of strong men. It is not a method of stagnant passivity. The phrase "passive resistance" often gives the false impression that this is a sort of "do nothing method" in which the resister quietly and passively accepts evil. But nothing is further from the truth. For while the nonviolent resister is passive in the sense that he is not physically aggressive toward his opponent, his mind and emotions are always active, constantly seeking to persuade his opponent that he is wrong. It is not passive non-resistance to evil; it is active nonviolent resistance to evil.

A second basic fact that characterizes nonviolence is that it does not seek to defeat or humiliate the opponent, but to win his friendship and understanding. The nonviolent resister must often express his protest through non-cooperation or boycotts, but he realizes that these are not ends themselves; they are merely means to awaken a sense of moral shame in the opponent. The end is redemption and reconciliation. The aftermath of nonviolence is the creation of the beloved community, while the aftermath of violence is tragic bitterness.

A third characteristic of this method is that the attack is directed against forces of evil rather than against persons who happen to be doing the evil. It is evil that the nonviolent resister seeks to defeat, not the persons victimized by evil. If he is opposing injustice, the nonviolent resister must have the vision to see the real and not the apparent antagonisms. As I have said again and again, to the people in Montgomery, "The tension is, at bottom between justice and injustice, between the forces of light and the forces of darkness. And if there is a victory, it will be a victory not merely of fifty thousand Negroes, but a victory for justice and the forces of light. We are out to defeat injustice and not white persons who may be unjust."

A fourth point that characterizes nonviolent resistance is a willingness to accept suffering without retaliation, to accept blows from the opponent without striking back. "Rivers of blood may have to flow before we gain our freedom, but it must be our blood," said Gandhi to his countrymen.[1] The non-violent resister is willing to accept violence if necessary, but never to inflict it. He does not seek to dodge jail. If going to jail is necessary, he enters it "as a bridegroom enters a bride's chamber."[2]

One may well ask: "What is the nonviolent resister's justification for this ordeal to which he invites men, for this mass political application of the ancient doctrine of turning the other cheek?" The answer is found in the realization that unearned suffering

---

1. This and the following footnote from Clayborne Carson et al., eds., *The Papers of Martin Luther King, Jr., Volume V: Threshold of a New Decade, January 1959–December 1960* (Berkeley: University of California Press, 2005), p. 124: "King's discussion of Gandhi in this draft may have been drawn from civil rights attorney Harris Wofford's address 'Nonviolence and the Law,' delivered at Howard University on 7 November 1957. Wofford: 'Rivers of blood may have to flow before we gain our freedom but it must be our blood,' he said to his countrymen. For an additional version of Wofford's address, see 'Nonviolence and the Law,' *Gandhi Marg* 3 (January 1959): 27–35. King had also relied on Wofford in his discussion of nonviolence in *Stride Toward Freedom.*"
2. "In Gandhi's 15 December 1921 'Young India' column, he wrote: 'We must widen the gates of prisons and we must enter them, as a bridegroom enters the bride's chamber' (*The Collected Works of Mahatma Gandhi*, vol. 22, December 1921–March 1922 [Delhi: Publications Division, Ministry of Information and Broadcasting, Government of India, 1971], p. 189)."

is redemptive. Suffering, the nonviolent resister realizes, has tremendous educational and transforming possibilities. "Things of fundamental importance to people are not secured by reason alone, but have to be purchased with their suffering," said Gandhi. He continues: "Suffering is infinitely more powerful than the law of the jungle for converting the opponent and opening his ears which are otherwise shut to the voice of reason. But beyond its effect upon the aggressor, the voluntary suffering inspires respect from the uncommitted and ultimately leads to a growth of, and solidarity with, the ranks of the peacemakers."

A fifth point concerning nonviolent resistance is that it avoids not only external physical violence but also internal violence of spirit. The nonviolent resister not only refuses to shoot his opponent but he also refuses to hate him. At the center of nonviolence stands the principle of love. The nonviolent resister would contend that in the struggle for human dignity, the oppressed people of the world must not succumb to the temptation of becoming bitter or indulging in hate campaigns. To retaliate in kind would do nothing but intensify the existence of hate in the universe. Along the way of life, someone must have sense enough and morality enough to cut off the chain of hate. This can only be done by projecting the ethic of love to the center of our lives.

On the eve of my departure for India, it is particularly appropriate that I have the privilege of being with the people who have had so long a dedicated concern for social justice, racial equality, and world peace. Let each of us go away this evening with a new determination to stand against the evils of our day. The challenge is here. To become the instruments of a great idea is a privilege that history gives only occasionally. Arnold Toynbee says in *A Study of History* that it may be the colored peoples who will give the new spiritual dynamic to western civilization that it so desperately needs to survive. I hope this is possible. The spiritual power that the colored peoples can radiate to the world comes from love, understanding, goodwill, and nonviolence. It may even be possible for the colored peoples through adherence to nonviolence so to challenge the nations of the world that they will seriously seek an alternative to war and destruction. In a day when Sputniks and Explorers dash through outer space and guided ballistic missiles are carving highways of death through the stratosphere, nobody can win a war. Today the choice is no longer between violence and nonviolence. It is either nonviolence or nonexistence. The colored peoples may be God's appeal to this age—an age drifting rapidly to its doom. The eternal appeal takes the form of a warning: "All who take the sword will perish by the sword."

"The Greatest Hope for World Peace"

Statements by Martin Luther King, Jr.

Prepared for *Redbook Magazine*

NOVEMBER 5, 1964

———◇———

On what do you most pin our hopes for world peace? And what, if anything, makes you most fearful of chances for peace?

MARTIN LUTHER KING, JR.: The greatest hope for world peace today may well be the realization on the part of people all over the world and the leaders of the nations of the world that war is futile. It may be through this rather negative path that we will come to a positive good for mankind. Recognition of the futility of warfare in an age where atomic and nuclear weapons can destroy the whole of mankind, may well be the thing that will bring about peace. Certainly in a day when Sputniks and Explorers are dashing through outer space, no nation can really win a war if it becomes a world war, and in this sense it is no longer a choice between violence and non-violence, but ultimately it will be non-violence or non-existence. The alternative to getting rid of war may be a civilization plunged into the abyss of annihilation. Now I think the greatest thing standing in the way of peace at this time is the existence of individuals often in power positions who have not recognized the danger of warfare. They have a sort of chip-on-the shoulder diplomacy, always inviting somebody to knock it off. It seems to me that if there is to be peace, the leaders of the world must recognize that despite political differences we've got to learn to live together. In short there must be peaceful coexistence or there will be co-annihilation.

Who are working most effectively for world peace today? And who seems most to be jeopardizing it?

MARTIN LUTHER KING, JR.: Many individuals in the United Nations from the Secretary General down are working very effectively and in a dedicated manner to bring about peace in the world. The United Nations has its faults, but certainly it is the best instrument we have at this time to bring about the dream of peace. Then there are those individuals who in various ways are constantly reminding their governments that disarmament must become a reality and that peace in the world must be the first item on the agenda of all nations of the world. These individuals are all working in a very creative manner. More and more religious institutions are coming to see the need for religion to take a stand on this issue. The World Council of Churches has made it very clear through recent proclamations and resolutions that war is immoral and that some alternative to it must be found. The same thing is true of the Roman Catholic Church and other religious bodies. I think the individuals who jeopardize peace are those who have not come to the point of seeing that the world must be made safe for diversity and that there must be the kind of give and take attitude necessary to bring about understanding. I also think peace is jeopardized by extreme nationalists who fail to see that in the world today we cannot live alone, that all the nations of the world are interdependent. No greater tragedy can befall the struggle for peace than the development of nations that feel they can live in monologue rather than dialogue, for the greatest channel to peace, it seems to me, is through dialogue—nations sitting down at the peace table talking together about problems that *must* continue to arise. For as long as we have men, we are going to have differences. And it seems to me we can disagree without being disagreeable.

Is war ever justifiable? Would you personally fight in self-defense?

MARTIN LUTHER KING, JR.: First, I am committed to non-violence absolutely, not merely as a technique or a passing strategy but as a way of life. For this reason I don't think I would fight in self-defense. I don't think that I would use violence in self-defense. Now on the question of whether war is ever justifiable, I have gone through the kind of intellectual pilgrimage on the whole question of war and the pacifist position and there was a period when I felt that war could serve a negative good—by that I mean I went through the feeling that war could at least serve as a force to block the surge of an evil force in history like Hitler, a misguided individual who is leading a nation and who can cause the destruction of many individuals. I never felt that war could be a positive good but I did think it could be a negative good in that it could prevent the flowering of a negative force in history. But now I have come to the conclusion that because of the potential annihilation of the whole human race, there can be no justification for any large scale war. And, I think the sooner men come to see that, the better off we will all be, and the better the future will be. In short, if man assumes that he has a right to survive, then he must find some substitute for war, and the sooner we come to see that war is obsolete and must be cast into unending limbo, the sooner we will develop the kind of world where we can all survive, and live together as brothers.

If you had omnipotent powers in your own country, or in the world, what would you do to promote the cause of permanent world peace?

MARTIN LUTHER KING, JR.: First, if I had this kind of omnipotent power, I would strengthen a channel that is already in existence, the United Nations. Through this channel I would seek to bring about a permanent test ban treaty all over the world so that there would be no testing in the atmosphere, subjecting us to the poison of radioactive fallout. Second, I would work to bring about universal disarmament and set up a world police force through the United Nations that could handle any problems that arise. I am not at all an anarchist, I believe in the intelligent use of police power, and I don't think man will ever come to the point where we will not need some checks. I would also consider some form of a world government. As we grow and come to see the oneness of mankind and the geographical oneness of the world, made possible by man's scientific and technological ingenuity, more and more we are going to have to try to see our oneness in terms of brotherhood. This does not mean that everyone has to agree at every point. There can be a world government where diversity can exist and this would lessen many tensions that we face today, and it would also enable everybody to understand that we are clothed in a single garment of destiny, and whatever affects one nation directly in the world, indirectly affects all.

"The Casualties of the War in Vietnam"

Speech by Martin Luther King, Jr.

The Nation Institute

Beverly-Hilton Hotel

LOS ANGELES, CALIFORNIA, FEBRUARY 25, 1967

I need not pause to say how happy I am to have the privilege of being a participant in this significant symposium. In these days of emotional tension when the problems of the world are gigantic in extent and chaotic in detail, there is no greater need than for sober-thinking, healthy debate, creative dissent and enlightened discussion. This is why this symposium is so important.

I would like to speak to you candidly and forthrightly this afternoon about our present involvement in Viet Nam. I have chosen as a subject, "The Casualties of the War in Viet Nam." We are all aware of the nightmarish physical casualties. We see them in our living rooms in all of their tragic dimensions on television screens, and we read about them on our subway and bus rides in daily newspaper accounts. We see the rice fields of a small Asian country being trampled at will and burned at whim: we see grief-stricken mothers with crying babies clutched in their arms as they watch their little huts burst forth into flames; we see the fields and valleys of battle being painted with humankind's blood; we see the broken bodies left prostrate in countless fields; we see young men being sent home half-men—physically handicapped and mentally deranged. Most tragic of all is the casualty list among children. Some one million Vietnamese children have been casualties of this brutal war. A war in which children are incinerated by napalm, in which American soldiers die in mounting numbers while other American soldiers, according to press accounts, in unrestrained hatred shoot the wounded enemy as they lie on the ground, is a war that mutilates the conscience. These casualties are enough to cause all men to rise up with righteous indignation and oppose the very nature of this war.

But the physical casualties of the war in Viet Nam are not alone the catastrophes. The casualties of principles and values are equally disastrous and injurious. Indeed, they are ultimately more harmful because they are self-perpetuating. If the casualties of principle are not healed, the physical casualties will continue to mount.

One of the first casualties of the war in Viet Nam was the Charter of the United Nations. In taking armed action against the Vietcong and North Viet Nam, the United States clearly violated the United Nations charter which provides, in chapter I, article II, "All members shall refrain in their international relations from the threat or use of force against the territorial integrity or political independence of any state or in any other manner inconsistent with the purposes of the United Nations"; and in chapter VII, "The Security Council shall determine the existence of any threat to the peace, breach of the peace, or act of aggression, and shall make recommendations or shall decide what measures shall be taken . . . to maintain or restore international peace and security."

It is very obvious that our government blatantly violated its obligation under the charter of the United Nations to submit to the Security Council its charge of aggression against North Viet Nam. Instead we unilaterally launched an all-out war on Asian soil. In the process we have undermined the purpose of the United Nations and caused its effectiveness to atrophy. We have also placed our nation in the position of being morally and politically isolated. Even the long standing allies of our nation have adamantly refused to join our government in this ugly war. As Americans and lovers of Democracy we should carefully ponder the consequences of our nation's declining moral status in the world.

The second casualty of the war in Viet Nam is the principle of self-determination. By entering a war that is little more than a domestic civil war, America has ended up supporting a new form of colonialism covered up by certain niceties of complexity. Whether we realize it or not our participation in the war in Viet Nam is an ominous expression of our lack of sympathy for the oppressed, our paranoid anti-Communism, our failure to feel the ache and anguish of the have nots. It reveals our willingness to continue participating in neo-colonialist adventures.

A brief look at the background and history of this war reveals with brutal clarity [the] ugliness of our policy. The Vietnamese people proclaimed their own independence in 1945 after a combined French and Japanese occupation, and before the Communist revolution in China. They were led by the now well-known Ho Chi Minh. Even though they quoted the American Declaration of Independence in their own document of freedom, we refused to recognize them. Instead, we decided to support France in its re-conquest of her former colony.

President Truman felt then that the Vietnamese people were not "ready" for independence, and we again fell victim to the deadly western arrogance that has poisoned the international atmosphere for so long. With that tragic decision we rejected a revolutionary government seeking self-determination, and a government that had been established not by China (for whom the Vietnamese have no great love) but by clearly indigenous forces that included some Communists.

For nine years following 1945 we denied the people of Viet Nam the right to independence. For nine years we vigorously supported the French in their abortive effort to re-colonize Viet Nam.

Before the end of the war we were meeting 80% of the French war costs. Even before the French were defeated at Dien Bien Phu, they began to despair of their reckless action, but we did not. We encouraged them with our huge financial and military supplies to continue the war even after they had lost the will.

During this period United States governmental officials began to brainwash the American public. John Foster Dulles assiduously sought to prove that Indo-China was essential to our security against the Chinese Communist peril. When a negotiated settlement of the war was reached in 1954, through the Geneva Accord, it was done against our will. After doing all that we could to sabotage the planning for the Geneva Accord, we finally refused to sign it.

Soon after this we helped install Ngo Dinh Diem. We supported him in his betrayal of the Geneva Accord and his refusal to have the promised 1956 election. We watched with approval as he engaged in ruthless and bloody persecution of all opposition forces. When Diem's infamous actions finally led to the formation of The National Liberation Front, the American public was duped into believing that the civil rebellion was being waged by puppets from Hanoi. As Douglas Pike wrote: "In horror, Americans helplessly watched Diem tear apart the fabric of Vietnamese society more effectively than the Communists had ever been able to do it. It was the most efficient act of his entire career."

Since Diem's death we have actively supported another dozen military dictatorships all in the name of fighting for freedom. When it became evident that these regimes could not defeat the Vietcong, we began to steadily increase our forces, calling them "military advisers" rather than fighting soldiers.

Today we are fighting an all-out war—undeclared by Congress. We have well over 300,000 American servicemen fighting in that benighted and unhappy country. American planes are bombing the territory of another country, and we are committing atrocities equal to any perpetrated by the Vietcong. This is the third largest war in American history.

All of this reveals that we are in an untenable position morally and politically. We are left standing before the world glutted by our barbarity. We are engaged in a war that seeks to turn the clock of history back and perpetuate white colonialism. The greatest irony and tragedy of all is that our nation which initiated so much of the revolutionary spirit of the modern world, is [now] cast in the mold of being an arch anti-revolutionary.

A third casualty of the war in Viet Nam is the Great Society. This confused war has played havoc with our domestic destinies.

Despite feeble protestations to the contrary, the promises of the Great Society have been shot down on the battlefield of Viet

Nam. The pursuit of this widened war has narrowed domestic welfare programs, making the poor, white and Negro, bear the heaviest burdens both at the front and at home.

While the anti-poverty program is cautiously initiated, zealously supervised and evaluated for immediate results, billions are liberally expended for this ill-considered war. The recently revealed mis-estimate of the war budget amounts to ten billions of dollars for a single year. This error alone is more than five times the amount committed to anti-poverty programs. The security we profess to seek in foreign adventures we will lose in our decaying cities. The bombs in Viet Nam explode at home: they destroy the hopes and possibilities for a decent America.

If we reversed investments and gave the armed forces the anti-poverty budget, the generals could be forgiven if they walked off the battlefield in disgust.

Poverty, urban problems and social progress generally are ignored when the guns of war become a national obsession. When it is not our security that is at stake, but questionable and vague commitments to reactionary regimes, values disintegrate into foolish and adolescent slogans.

It is estimated that we spend $322,000 for each enemy we kill, while we spend in the so-called war on poverty in America only about $53.00 for each person classified as "poor." And much of that 53 dollars goes for salaries of people who are not poor. We have escalated the war in Viet Nam and de-escalated the skirmish against poverty. It challenges the imagination to contemplate what lives we could transform if we were to cease killing.

At this moment in history it is irrefutable that our world prestige is pathetically frail. Our war policy excites pronounced contempt and aversion virtually everywhere. Even when some national governments, for reasons of economic and diplomatic interest, do not condemn us, their people in surprising measure have made clear they do not share the official policy.

We are isolated in our false values in a world demanding social and economic justice. We must undergo a vigorous re-ordering of our national priorities.

A fourth casualty of the war in Viet Nam is the humility of our nation. Through rugged determination, scientific and technological progress and dazzling achievements, America has become the richest and most powerful nation in the world. We have built machines that think and instruments that peer into the unfathomable ranges of interstellar space. We have built gargantuan bridges to span the seas and gigantic buildings to kiss the skies. Through our airplanes and spaceships we have dwarfed distance and placed time in chains, and through our submarines we have penetrated oceanic depths. This year our national gross product will reach the astounding figure of 780 billion dollars. All of this is a staggering picture of our great power.

But honesty impels me to admit that our power has often made us arrogant. We feel that our money can do anything. We arrogantly feel that we have everything to teach other nations and nothing to learn from them. We often arrogantly feel that we have some divine, messianic mission to police the whole world. We are arrogant in not allowing young nations to go through the same growing pains, turbulence and revolution that characterized our history. We are arrogant in our contention that we have some sacred mission to protect people from totalitarian rule, while we make little use of our power to end the evils of South Africa and Rhodesia, and while we are in fact supporting dictatorships with guns and money under the guise of fighting Communism. We are arrogant in professing to be concerned about the freedom of foreign nations while not setting our own house in order. Many of our Senators and Congressmen vote joyously to appropriate billions of dollars for war in Viet Nam, and these same Senators and Congressmen vote loudly against a Fair Housing Bill to make it possible for a Negro veteran of Viet Nam to purchase a decent home. We arm Negro soldiers to kill on foreign battlefields, but offer little protection for their relatives from beatings and killings in our own south. We are willing to make the Negro 100% of a citizen in warfare, but reduce him to 50% of a citizen on American soil. Of all the good things in life the Negro has approximately one half those of whites; of the bad he has twice that of whites. Thus, half of all Negroes live in substandard housing and Negroes have half the income of whites. When we turn to the negative experiences of life, the Negro has a double share. There are twice as many unemployed. The infant mortality rate is double that of white. There are twice as many Negroes in combat in Viet Nam at the beginning of 1967 and twice as many died in action (20.6%) in proportion to their numbers in the population as whites.

All of this reveals that our nation has not yet used its vast resources of power to end the long night of poverty, racism and man's inhumanity to man. Enlarged power means enlarged peril if there is not concomitant growth of the soul. Genuine power is the right use of strength. If our nation's strength is not used responsibly and with restraint, it will be, following Acton's dictum, power that tends to corrupt and absolute power that corrupts absolutely. Our arrogance can be our doom. It can bring the curtains down on our national drama. Ultimately a great nation is a compassionate nation. We are challenged in these turbulent days to use our power to speed up the day when "every valley shall be exalted, and every mountain and hill shall be made low: and the crooked shall be made straight, and the rough places plain."

A fifth casualty of the war in Viet Nam is the principle of dissent. An ugly repressive sentiment to silence peace-seekers depicts advocates of immediate negotiation under terms of the Geneva agreement and persons who call for a cessation of bombings in the north as quasi-traitors, fools or venal enemies of our soldiers and institutions. Free speech and the privilege of dissent and discussion are rights being shot down by bombers in Viet Nam. When those who stand for peace are so vilified it is time to consider where we are going and whether free speech has not become one of the major casualties of the war.

Curtailment of free speech is rationalized on grounds that a more compelling American tradition forbids criticism of the government when the nation is at war. More than a century ago when we were in a declared state of war with Mexico, a first term congressman by the name of Abraham Lincoln stood in the halls of

Congress and fearlessly denounced that war. Congressman Abraham Lincoln of Illinois had not heard of this tradition or he was not inclined to respect it. Nor had Thoreau and Emerson and many other philosophers who shaped our democratic principles. Nothing can be more destructive of our fundamental democratic traditions than the vicious effort to silence dissenters.

A sixth casualty of the war in Viet Nam is the prospects of mankind's survival. This war has created the climate for greater armament and further expansion of destructive nuclear power.

One of the most persistent ambiguities that we face is that everybody talks about peace as a goal. However, it does not take sharpest-eyed sophistication to discern that while everybody talks about peace, peace has become practically nobody's business among the power-wielders. Many men cry peace! peace! but they refuse to do the things that make for peace.

The large power blocs of the world talk passionately of pursuing peace while burgeoning defense budgets that already bulge, enlarging already awesome armies, and devising even more devastating weapons. Call the roll of those who sing the glad tidings of peace and one's ears will be surprised by the responding sounds. The heads of all of the nations issue clarion calls for peace yet these destiny determiners come accompanied by a band and a brigand of national choristers, each bearing unsheathed swords rather than olive branches.

The stages of history are replete with the chants and choruses of the conquerors of old who came killing in pursuit of peace. Alexander, Genghis Khan, Julius Caesar, Charlemagne, and Napoleon were akin in their seeking a peaceful world order, a world fashioned after their selfish conceptions of an ideal existence. Each sought a world at peace which would personify his egotistic dreams. Even within the life span of most of us, another megalomaniac strode across the world stage. He sent his blitzkrieg-bent legions blazing across Europe, bringing havoc and holocaust in his wake. There is grave irony in the fact that Hitler could come forth, following the nakedly aggressive expansionist theories he revealed in *Mein Kampf*, and do it all in the name of peace.

So when I see in this day the leaders of nations similarly talking peace while preparing for war, I take frightful pause. When I see our country today intervening in what is basically a civil war, destroying hundreds of thousands of Vietnamese children with Napalm, leaving broken bodies in countless fields and sending home half-men, mutilated, mentally and physically; when I see the recalcitrant unwillingness of our government to create the atmosphere for a negotiated settlement of this awful conflict by halting bombings in the north and agreeing to talk with the Vietcong— and all this in the name of pursuing the goal of peace—I tremble for our world. I do so not only from dire recall of the nightmares wreaked in the wars of yesterday, but also from dreadful realization of today's possible nuclear destructiveness, and tomorrow's even more damnable prospects.

In the light of all this, I say that we must narrow the gaping chasm between our proclamations of peace and our lowly deeds which precipitate and perpetuate war. We are called upon to look up from the quagmire of military programs and defense commitments and read history's signposts and today's trends.

The past is prophetic in that it asserts loudly that wars are poor chisels for carving out peaceful tomorrows. One day we must come to see that peace is not merely a distant goal that we seek, but a means by which we arrive at that goal. We must pursue peaceful ends through peaceful means. How much longer must we play at deadly war games before we heed the plaintive pleas of the unnumbered dead and maimed of past wars? Why can't we at long last grow up, and take off our blindfolds, chart new courses, put our hands to the rudder and set sail for the distant destination, the port city of peace?

President John F. Kennedy said on one occasion, "Mankind must put an end to war or war will put an end to mankind." Wisdom born of experience should tell us that war is obsolete. There may have been a time when war served as a negative good by preventing the spread and growth of an evil force, but the destructive power of modern weapons eliminates even the possibility that war may serve as a negative good. If we assume that life is worth living and that man has a right to survive, then we must find an alternative to war. In a day when vehicles hurtle through outer space and guided ballistic missiles carve highways of death through the stratosphere, no nation can claim victory in war. A so-called limited war will leave little more than a calamitous legacy of human suffering, political turmoil, and spiritual disillusionment. A world war—God forbid!—will leave only smoldering ashes as a mute testimony of a human race whose folly led inexorably to ultimate death. So if modern man continues to flirt unhesitatingly with war, he will transform his earthly habitat into an inferno such as even the mind of Dante could not imagine.

I do not wish to minimize the complexity of the problems that need to be faced in achieving disarmament and peace. But I think it is a fact that we shall not have the will, the courage and the insight to deal with such matters unless in this field we are prepared to undergo a mental and spiritual re-evaluation, a change of focus which will enable us to see that the things which seem most real and powerful are indeed now unreal and have come under the sentence of death. We need to make a supreme effort to generate the readiness, indeed the eagerness, to enter into the new world which is now possible.

We will not build a peaceful world by following a negative path. It is not enough to say "we must not wage war." It is necessary to love peace and sacrifice for it. We must concentrate not merely on the negative expulsion of war, but on the positive affirmation of peace. There is a fascinating little story that is preserved for us in Greek literature about Ulysses and the Sirens. The Sirens had the ability to sing so sweetly that sailors could not resist steering toward their island. Many ships were lured upon the rocks and the men forgot home, duty and honor as they flung themselves into the sea to be embraced by arms that drew them down to death. Ulysses, determined not to be lured by the Sirens, first decided to tie himself tightly to the mast of his boat and his crew stuffed their ears with wax. But finally he and his crew learned a better way to save themselves: they took on board the beautiful singer Orpheus whose melodies were sweeter than the music of the Sirens. When Orpheus sang, who bothered to listen to the Sirens? So we must fix our visions not merely on the negative expulsion of war but upon the positive affirmation of peace. We must see that peace represents a sweeter music, a cosmic melody that is far superior to the discords of war. Somehow we must transform the dynamics of the world power struggle from the negative nuclear arms race which no one can win to a positive contest to harness man's creative genius for the purpose of making peace and prosperity a reality for all of the nations of the world. In short, we must shift the arms race into a "peace race." If we have the will and determination to mount such a peace offensive we will unlock hitherto tightly sealed doors of hope and bring new light into the dark chambers of pessimism.

Let me say finally that I oppose the war in Viet Nam because I love America. I speak out against it not in anger but with anxiety and sorrow in my heart, and above all with a passionate desire to see our beloved country stand as the moral example of the world. I speak out against this war because I am disappointed with America. There can be no great disappointment where there is no great love. I am disappointed with our failure to deal positively and forthrightly with the triple evils of racism, extreme materialism and militarism. We are presently moving down a dead-end road that can lead to national disaster.

Jesus once told a parable of a young man who left home and wandered into a far country where, in adventure after adventure and sensation after sensation, he sought life. But he never found it; he found only frustration and bewilderment. The farther he moved from his father's house, the closer he came to the house of despair. The more he did what he liked, the less he liked what he did. After the boy had wasted all, a famine developed in the land, and he ended up seeking food in a pig's trough. But the story does not end there. It goes on to say that in this state of disillusionment, blinding frustration and homesickness, the boy "came to himself" and said, "I will arise and go to my father, and will say to him, Father, I have sinned against heaven and before thee." The prodigal son was not himself when he left his father's house or when he dreamed that pleasure was the end of life. Only when he made up his mind to go home and be a son again did he really come to himself. The parable ends with the boy returning home to find a loving father waiting with outstretched arms and heart filled with unutterable joy.

This is an analogy of what America confronts today. Like all human analogies, it is imperfect, but it does suggest some parallels worth considering. America has strayed to the far country of racism and militarism. The home that all too many Americans left was solidly structured idealistically. Its pillars were soundly grounded in the insights of our Judeo-Christian heritage—all men are made in the image of God; all men are brothers; all men are created equal; every man is heir to a legacy of dignity and worth; every man has rights that are neither conferred by nor derived from the state, they are God-given; out of one blood God made all men to dwell upon the face of the earth. What a marvelous foundation for any home! What a glorious and healthy place to inhabit! But America strayed away; and this unnatural excursion has brought only confusion and bewilderment. It has left hearts aching with guilt and minds distorted with irrationality. It has driven wisdom from her sacred throne. This long and callous sojourn in the far country of racism and militarism has brought a moral and spiritual famine to the nation.

It is time for all people of conscience to call upon America to return to her true home of brotherhood and peaceful pursuits. We cannot remain silent as our nation engages in one of history's most cruel and senseless wars. America must continue to have, during these days of human travail, a company of creative dissenters. We need them because the thunder of their fearless voices will be the only sound stronger than the blasts of bombs and the clamour of war hysteria.

Those of us who love peace must organize as effectively as the war hawks. As they spread the propaganda of war we must spread the propaganda of peace. We must combine the fervor of the civil rights movement with the peace movement. We must demonstrate, teach and preach, until the very foundations of our nation are shaken. We must work unceasingly to lift this nation that we love to a higher destiny, to a new plateau of compassion, to a more noble expression of humane-ness.

I have tried to be honest today. To be honest is to confront the truth. To be honest is to realize that the ultimate measure of a man is not where he stands in moments of convenience and moments of comfort, but where he stands in moments of challenge and moments of controversy. However unpleasant and inconvenient the truth may be, I believe we must expose and face it if we are to achieve a better quality of American life.

Just the other day, the distinguished American historian, Henry Steele Commager, told a Senate Committee: "Justice Holmes used to say that the first lesson a judge had to learn was that he was not God . . . we do tend perhaps more than other nations, to transform our wars into crusades . . . our current involvement in Viet Nam is cast, increasingly, into a moral mold . . . It is my feeling that we do not have the resources, material, intellectual or moral, to be at once an American power, a European power and an Asian power."

I agree with Mr. Commager. And I would suggest that there is, however, another kind of power that America can and should be. It is a moral power, a power harnessed to the service of peace and human beings, not an inhumane power unleashed against defenseless people. All the world knows that America is a great military power. We need not be diligent in seeking to prove it. We must now show the world our moral power.

There is an element of urgency in our re-directing American power. We are now faced with the fact that tomorrow is today. We are confronted with the fierce urgency of *now*. In this unfolding conundrum of life and history there is such a thing as being too late. Procrastination is still the thief of time. Life often leaves us standing bare, naked, and dejected with a lost opportunity. The "tide in the affairs of men" does not remain at flood: it ebbs. We may cry out desperately for time to pause in her passage, but time is adamant to every plea and rushes on. Over the bleached bones and jumbled residue of numerous civilizations are written the pathetic words: "Too late." There is an invisible book of life that faithfully records our vigilance or our neglect. "The moving finger writes, and having writ moves on . . ." We still have a choice today: nonviolent co-existence or violent co-annihilation. History will record the choice we made. It is still not too late to make the proper choice. If we decide to become a moral power we will be able to transform the jangling discords of this world into a beautiful symphony of brotherhood. If we make the wise decision we will be able to transform our pending cosmic elegy into a creative psalm of peace. This will be a glorious day. In reaching it we can fulfill the noblest of American dreams.

"Beyond Vietnam:
A Time to Break Silence"

Speech by Martin Luther King, Jr.

Clergy and Laity Concerned About Vietnam (CALC)

Riverside Church

NEW YORK, NEW YORK, APRIL 4, 1967

I come to this magnificent house of worship tonight because my conscience leaves me no other choice. I join you in this meeting because I am in deepest agreement with the aims and work of the organization which has brought us together: Clergy and [Laity] Concerned About Vietnam. The recent statement of your executive committee are the sentiments of my own heart and I found myself in full accord when I read its opening lines: "A time comes when silence is betrayal." That time has come for us in relation to Vietnam.

The truth of these words is beyond doubt, but the mission to which they call us is a most difficult one. Even when pressed by the demands of inner truth, men do not easily assume the task of opposing their government's policy, especially in time of war. Nor does the human spirit move without great difficulty against all the apathy of conformist thought within one's own bosom and in the surrounding world. Moreover when the issues at hand seem as perplexing as they often do in the case of this dreadful conflict we are always on the verge of being mesmerized by uncertainty: but we must move on.

Some of us who have already begun to break the silence of the night have found that the calling to speak is often a vocation of agony, but we must speak. We must speak with all the humility that is appropriate to our limited vision, but we must speak. And we must rejoice as well, for surely this is the first time in our nation's history that a significant number of its religious leaders have chosen to move beyond the prophesying of smooth patriotism to the high grounds of a firm dissent based upon the mandates of conscience and the reading of history. Perhaps a new spirit is rising among us. If it is, let us trace its movements well and pray that our own inner being may be sensitive to its guidance, for we are deeply in need of a new way beyond the darkness that seems so close around us.

Over the past two years, as I have moved to break the betrayal of my own silences and to speak from the burnings of my own heart, as I have called for radical departures from the destruction of Vietnam, many persons have questioned me about the wisdom of my path. At the heart of their concerns this query has often loomed large and loud: Why are *you* speaking about the war, Dr. King? Why are *you* joining the voices of dissent? Peace and civil rights don't mix, they say. Aren't you hurting the cause of your people, they ask? And when I hear them, though I often understand the sources of their concern, I am nevertheless greatly saddened, for such questions mean that the inquirers have not really known me, my commitment or my calling. Indeed, their questions suggest that they do not know the world in which they live.

In the light of such tragic misunderstanding, I deem it of signal importance to try to state clearly, and I trust concisely, why I believe that the path from Dexter Avenue Baptist Church—the church in Montgomery, Alabama where I began my pastorate— leads clearly to this sanctuary tonight.

I come to this platform tonight to make a passionate plea to my beloved nation. This speech is not addressed to Hanoi or to the National Liberation Front. It is not addressed to China or to Russia.

Nor is it an attempt to overlook the ambiguity of the total situation and the need for a collective solution to the tragedy of Vietnam. Neither is it an attempt to make North Vietnam or the National Liberation Front paragons of virtue, nor to overlook the role they can play in a successful resolution of the problem. While they both may have justifiable reason to be suspicious of the good faith of the United States, life and history give eloquent testimony to the fact that conflicts are never resolved without trustful give and take on both sides.

Tonight, however, I wish not to speak with Hanoi and the NLF, but rather to my fellow Americans who, with me, bear the greatest responsibility in ending a conflict that has exacted a heavy price on both continents.

Since I am a preacher by trade, I suppose it is not surprising that I have several reasons for bringing Vietnam into the field of my moral vision. There is at the outset a very obvious and almost facile connection between the war in Vietnam and the struggle I, and others, have been waging in America. A few years ago there was a shining moment in that struggle. It seemed as if there was a real promise of hope for the poor—both black and white—through the Poverty Program. There were experiments, hopes, new beginnings. Then came the build-up in Vietnam and I watched the program broken and eviscerated as if it were some idle political plaything of a society gone mad on war, and I knew that America would never invest the necessary funds or energies in rehabilitation of its poor so long as adventures like Vietnam continued to draw men and skills and money like some demoniacal destructive suction tube. So I was increasingly compelled to see the war as an enemy of the poor and to attack it as such.

Perhaps the more tragic recognition of reality took place when it became clear to me that the war was doing far more than devastating the hopes of the poor at home. It was sending their sons and their brothers and their husbands to fight and to die in extraordinarily high proportions relative to the rest of the population. We were taking the black young men who had been crippled by our society and sending them 8,000 miles away to guarantee liberties in Southeast Asia which they had not found in Southwest Georgia and East Harlem. So we have been repeatedly faced with the cruel irony of watching Negro and white boys on TV screens as they kill and die together for a nation that has been unable to seat them together in the same schools. So we watch them in brutal solidarity burning the huts of a poor village but we realize that they would never live on the same block in Detroit. I could not be silent in the face of such cruel manipulation of the poor.

My third reason moves to an even deeper level of awareness, for it grows out of my experience in the ghettos of the north over the last three years—especially the last three summers. As I have walked among the desperate, rejected and angry young men I have told them that Molotov cocktails and rifles would not solve their problems. I have tried to offer them my deepest compassion while maintaining my conviction that social change comes most meaningfully through non-violent action. But they asked—and rightly so—what about Vietnam? They asked if our own nation wasn't using massive doses of violence to solve its problems, to bring about the changes it wanted. Their questions hit home, and I knew that I could never again raise my voice against the violence of the oppressed in the ghettos without having first spoken clearly to the greatest purveyor of violence in the world today—my own government. For the sake of those boys, for the sake of this government, for the sake of the hundreds of thousands trembling under our violence, I cannot be silent.

For those who ask the question, "Aren't you a Civil Rights leader?" and thereby mean to exclude me from the movement for peace, I have this further answer. In 1957 when a group of us formed the Southern Christian Leadership Conference, we chose as our motto: "To save the soul of America." We were convinced that we could not limit our vision to certain rights for black people, but instead affirmed the conviction that America would never be free or saved from itself unless the descendants of its slaves were loosed completely from the shackles they still wear. In a way we were agreeing with Langston Hughes, that black bard of Harlem, who had written earlier:

> O, yes,
> I say it plain,
> America never was America to me,
> And yet I swear this oath—
> America will be!

Now, it should be incandescently clear that no one who has any concern for the integrity and life of America today can ignore the present war. If America's soul becomes totally poisoned, part of the autopsy must read Vietnam. It can never be saved so long as it destroys the deepest hopes of men the world over. So it is that those of us who are yet determined that America *will* be are led down the path of protest and dissent, working for the health of our land.

As if the weight of such a commitment to the life and health of America were not enough, another burden of responsibility was placed upon me in 1964; and I cannot forget that the Nobel Prize for Peace was also a commission—a commission to work harder than I had ever worked before for "the brotherhood of man." This is a calling that takes me beyond national allegiances, but even if it were not present I would yet have to live with the meaning of my commitment to the ministry of Jesus Christ. To me the relationship of this ministry to the making of peace is so obvious that I sometimes marvel at those who ask me why I am speaking against the war. Could it be that they do not know that the good news was meant for all men—for communist and capitalist, for their children and ours, for black and for white, for revolutionary and conservative? Have they forgotten that my ministry is in obedience to the one who loved his enemies so fully that he died for them? What then can I say to the Vietcong or to Castro or to Mao as a faithful minister of this one? Can I threaten them with death or must I not share with them my life?

Finally, as I try to delineate for you and for myself the road that leads from Montgomery to this place I would have offered all that was most valid if I simply said that I must be true to my conviction that I share with all men the calling to be a son of the Living God. Beyond the calling of race or nation or creed is this vocation of sonship and brotherhood, and because I believe that the Father is deeply concerned especially for his suffering and helpless and outcast children, I come tonight to speak for them.

This I believe to be the privilege and the burden of all of us who deem ourselves bound by allegiances and loyalties which are broader and deeper than nationalism and which go beyond our nation's self-defined goals and positions. We are called to speak for the weak, for the voiceless, for victims of our nation and for those it calls enemy, for no document from human hands can make these humans any less our brothers.

And as I ponder the madness of Vietnam and search within myself for ways to understand and respond in compassion my mind goes constantly to the people of that peninsula. I speak now not of the soldiers of each side, not of the junta in Saigon, but simply of the people who have been living under the curse of war for almost three continuous decades now. I think of them too because it is clear to me that there will be no meaningful solution there until some attempt is made to know them and hear their broken cries.

They must see Americans as strange liberators. The Vietnamese people proclaimed their own independence in 1945 after a combined French and Japanese occupation, and before the communist revolution in China. They were led by Ho Chi Minh. Even though they quoted the American Declaration of Independence in their own document of freedom, we refused to recognize them. Instead, we decided to support France in its re-conquest of her former colony.

Our government felt then that the Vietnamese people were not "ready" for independence, and we again fell victim to the deadly western arrogance that has poisoned the international atmosphere for so long. With that tragic decision we rejected a revolutionary government seeking self-determination, and a government that had been established not by China (for whom the Vietnamese have no great love) but by clearly indigenous forces that included some communists. For the peasants this new government meant real land reform, one of the most important needs in their lives.

For nine years following 1945 we denied the people of Vietnam the right of independence. For nine years we vigorously supported the French in their abortive effort to re-colonize Vietnam.

Before the end of the war we were meeting 80% of the French war costs. Even before the French were defeated at Dien Bien Phu, they began to despair of the reckless action, but we did not. We encouraged them with our huge financial and military supplies to continue the war even after they had lost the will. Soon we would be paying almost the full costs of this tragic attempt at re-colonization.

After the French were defeated it looked as if independence and land reform would come again through the Geneva agreements. But instead there came the United States, determined that Ho should not unify the temporarily divided nation, and the peasants watched again as we supported one of the most vicious modern dictators—our chosen man, Premier Diem. The peasants watched and cringed as Diem ruthlessly routed out all opposition, supported their extortionist landlords and refused even to discuss re-unification with the North. The peasants watched as all this was presided over by U.S. influence and then by increasing numbers of U.S. troops who came to help quell the insurgency that Diem's methods had aroused. When Diem was overthrown they may have been happy, but the long line of military dictatorships seemed to offer no real change—especially in terms of their need for land and peace.

The only change came from America as we increased our troop commitments in support of governments which were singularly corrupt, inept and without popular support. All the while the people read our leaflets and received regular promises of peace and democracy—and land reform. Now they languish under our bombs and consider us—not their fellow Vietnamese—the real enemy. They move sadly and apathetically as we herd them off the land of their fathers into concentration camps where minimal social needs are rarely met. They know they must move or be destroyed by our bombs. So they go—primarily women and children and the aged.

They watch as we poison their water, as we kill a million acres of their crops. They must weep as the bulldozers roar through their areas preparing to destroy the precious trees. They wander into the hospitals, with at least 20 casualties from American firepower for one Vietcong-inflicted injury. They wander into the towns and see thousands of the children, homeless, without clothes, running in packs on the streets like animals. They see the children degraded by our soldiers as they beg for food. They see the children selling their sisters to our soldiers, soliciting for their mothers.

What do the peasants think as we ally ourselves with the landlords and as we refuse to put any action into our many words concerning land reform? What do they think as we test out our latest weapons on them, just as the Germans tested out new medicine and new tortures in the concentration camps of Europe? Where are the roots of the independent Vietnam we claim to be building? Is it among these voiceless ones?

We have destroyed their two most cherished institutions: the family and the village. We have destroyed their land and their crops. We have cooperated in the crushing of the nation's only non-communist revolutionary political force—the unified Buddhist Church. We have supported the enemies of the peasants of Saigon. We have corrupted their women and children and killed their men. What liberators!

Now there is little left to build on—save bitterness. Soon the only solid physical foundations remaining will be found at our military bases and in the concrete of the concentration camps we call fortified hamlets. The peasants may well wonder if we plan to build our new Vietnam on such grounds as these? Could we blame them for such thoughts? We must speak for them and raise the questions they cannot raise. These too are our brothers.

Perhaps the more difficult but no less necessary task is to speak for those who have been designated as our enemies. What of the National Liberation Front—that strangely anonymous group we call VC or Communists? What must they think of us in America when they realize that we permitted the repression and cruelty of Diem which helped to bring them into being as a resistance group in the south? What do they think of our condoning the violence which led to their own taking up of arms? How can they believe in our integrity when now we speak of "aggression from the North" as if there were nothing more essential to the war?

How can they trust us when now we charge them with violence after the murderous reign of Diem, and charge them with violence while we pour every new weapon of death into their land? Surely we must understand their feelings even if we do not condone their actions. Surely we must see that the men we supported pressed them to their violence. Surely we must see that our own computerized plans of destruction simply dwarf their greatest acts.

How do they judge us when our officials know that their membership is less than 25 per cent communist and yet insist on giving them the blanket name? What must they be thinking when they know that we are aware of their control of major sections of Vietnam and yet we appear ready to allow national elections in which this highly organized political parallel government will have no part? They ask how we can speak of free elections when the Saigon press is censored and controlled by the military junta. And they are surely right to wonder what kind of new government we plan to help form without them—the only party in real touch with the peasants. They question our political goals and they deny the reality of a peace settlement from which they will be excluded. Their questions are frighteningly relevant. Is our nation planning to build on political myth again and then shore it up with the power of new violence?

Here is the true meaning and value of compassion and nonviolence when it helps us to see the enemy's point of view, to hear his questions, to know his assessment of ourselves. For from his view we may indeed see the basic weaknesses of our own condition, and if we are mature, we may learn and grow and profit from the wisdom of the brothers who are called the opposition.

So, too, with Hanoi. In the North, where our bombs now pummel the land, and our mines endanger the waterways, we are met by a deep but understandable mistrust. To speak for them is to explain this lack of confidence in western words, and especially their distrust of American intentions now. In Hanoi are the men who led the nation to independence against the Japanese and the French, the men who sought membership in the French commonwealth and were betrayed by the weakness of Paris and the willfulness of the colonial armies. It was they who led a second struggle against French domination at tremendous costs, and then were persuaded to give up the land they controlled between the 13th and 17th parallel as a temporary measure at Geneva. After 1954 they watched us conspire with Diem to prevent elections which would have surely brought Ho Chi Minh to power over a united Vietnam, and they realized they had been betrayed again.

When we ask why they do not leap to negotiate, these things must be remembered. Also it must be clear that the leaders of Hanoi considered the presence of American troops in support of the Diem regime to have been the initial military breach of the Geneva Agreements concerning foreign troops, and they remind us that they did not begin to send in any large number of supplies or men until American forces had moved into the tens of thousands.

Hanoi remembers how our leaders refused to tell us the truth about the earlier North Vietnamese overtures for peace, how we claimed that none existed when they had clearly been made. Ho Chi Minh has watched as America has spoken of peace and built up its forces, and now he has surely heard the increasing international rumors of American plans for an invasion of the North. Perhaps only his sense of humor and irony can save him when he hears the most powerful nation of the world speaking of *his* aggression as it drops thousands of bombs on a poor weak nation more than 8,000 miles away from its shores.

At this point I should make it clear that while I have tried in these last few minutes to give a voice to the voiceless on Vietnam and to understand the arguments of those who are called enemy, I am as deeply concerned about our own troops there as anything else. For it occurs to me that what we are submitting them to in Vietnam is not simply the brutalizing process that goes on in any war where armies face each other and seek to destroy. We are adding cynicism to the process of death, for they must know after a short period there that none of the things we claim to be fighting for are really involved. Before long they must know that their government has sent them into a struggle among Vietnamese, and the more sophisticated surely realize that we are on the side of the wealthy and the secure while we create a hell for the poor.

Somehow this madness must cease. We must stop now. I speak as a child of God and brother to the suffering poor of Vietnam. I speak for those whose land is being laid waste, whose homes are being destroyed, whose culture is being subverted. I speak for the poor of America who are paying the double price of smashed hopes at home and death and corruption in Vietnam. I speak as a citizen of the world, for the world as it stands aghast at the path we have taken. I speak as an American to the leaders of my own nation. The great initiative in this war is ours. The initiative to stop it must be ours.

This is the message of the great Buddhist leaders of Vietnam. Recently one of them wrote these words: "Each day the war goes on, the hatred increases in the heart of the Vietnamese and in the hearts of those of humanitarian instinct. The Americans are forcing even their friends into becoming their enemies. It is curious that the Americans, who calculate so carefully on the possibilities of military victory, do not realize that in the process they are incurring deep psychological and political defeat. The image of America will never again be the image of revolution, freedom and democracy, but the image of violence and militarism."

If we continue there will be no doubt in my mind and in the mind of the world that we have no honorable intentions in Vietnam. It will become clear that our minimal expectation is to occupy it as an American colony and men will not refrain from thinking that our maximum hope is to goad China into a war so that we may bomb her nuclear installations. If we do not stop our war against the people of Vietnam immediately the world will be left with no other alternative than to see this as some horribly clumsy and deadly game we have decided to play.

The world now demands a maturity of America that we may not be able to achieve. It demands that we admit that we have been wrong from the beginning of our adventure in Vietnam, that we have been detrimental to the life of the Vietnamese people.

In order to atone for our sins and errors in Vietnam, we should take the initiative in bringing a halt to this tragic war. I would like to suggest five concrete things that our government should do immediately to begin the long and difficult process of extricating ourselves from this nightmarish conflict:

1. End all bombing in North and South Vietnam.
2. Declare a unilateral cease-fire in the hope that such action will create the atmosphere for negotiation.
3. Take immediate steps to prevent other battlegrounds in Southeast Asia by curtailing our military build-up in Thailand and our interference in Laos.
4. Realistically accept the fact that the National Liberation Front has substantial support in South Vietnam and must thereby play a role in any meaningful negotiations and in any future Vietnam government.
5. Set a date that we will remove all foreign troops from Vietnam in accordance with the 1954 Geneva Agreement.

Part of our ongoing commitment might well express itself in an offer to grant asylum to any Vietnamese who fears for his life under a new regime which included the Liberation Front. Then we must make what reparations we can for the damage we have done. We must provide the medical aid that is badly needed, making it available in this country if necessary.

Meanwhile we in the churches and synagogues have a continuing task while we urge our government to disengage itself from a disgraceful commitment. We must continue to raise our voices if our nation persists in its perverse ways in Vietnam. We must be prepared to match actions with words by seeking out every creative means of protest possible.

As we counsel young men concerning military service we must clarify for them our nation's role in Vietnam and challenge them with the alternative of conscientious objection. I am pleased to say that this is the path now being chosen by more than seventy students at my own Alma Mater, Morehouse College, and I recommend it to all who find the American course in Vietnam a dishonorable and unjust one. Moreover I would encourage all ministers of draft age to give up their ministerial exemptions and seek status as conscientious objectors. These are the times for real choices and not false ones. We are at the moment when our lives must be placed on the line if our nation is to survive its own folly. Every man of humane convictions must decide on the protest that best suits his convictions, but we must all protest.

There is something seductively tempting about stopping there and sending us all off on what in some circles has become a popular crusade against the war in Vietnam. I say we must enter that struggle, but I wish to go on now to say something even more disturbing. The war in Vietnam is but a symptom of a far deeper malady within the American spirit, and if we ignore this sobering reality we will find ourselves organizing clergy and laymen-concerned committees for the next generation. They will be concerned about Guatemala and Peru. They will be concerned about Thailand and Cambodia. They will be concerned about Mozambique and South Africa. We will be marching for these and a dozen other names and attending rallies without end unless there is a significant and profound change in American life and policy. Such thoughts take us beyond Vietnam, but not beyond our calling as sons of the living God.

In 1957 a sensitive American official overseas said that it seemed to him that our nation was on the wrong side of a world revolution. During the past 10 years we have seen emerge a pattern of suppression which now has justified the presence of U.S. military "advisors" in Venezuela. This need to maintain social stability for our investments accounts for the counter-revolutionary action of American forces in Guatemala. It tells why American helicopters are being used against guerrillas in Colombia and why American napalm and green beret forces have already been active against rebels in Peru. It is with such activity in mind that the words of the late John F. Kennedy come back to haunt us. Five years ago he said, "Those who make peaceful revolution impossible will make violent revolution inevitable."

Increasingly, by choice or by accident, this is the role our nation has taken—the role of those who make peaceful revolution impossible by refusing to give up the privileges and the pleasures that come from the immense profits of overseas investment.

I am convinced that if we are to get on the right side of the world revolution, we as a nation must undergo a radical revolution of values. We must rapidly begin the shift from a "thing-oriented" society to a "person-oriented" society. When machines and computers, profit motives and property rights are considered more important than people, the giant triplets of racism, materialism, and militarism are incapable of being conquered.

A true revolution of values will soon cause us to question the fairness and justice of many of our past and present policies. On the one hand we are called to play the Good Samaritan on life's roadside; but that will be only an initial act. One day we must come to see that the whole Jericho Road must be transformed so that men and women will not be constantly beaten and robbed as they make their journey on Life's highway. True compassion is more than flinging a coin to a beggar; it is not haphazard and superficial. It comes to see that an edifice which produces beggars needs re-structuring. A true revolution of values will soon look uneasily on the glaring contrast of poverty and wealth. With righteous indignation, it will look across the seas and see individual capitalists of the West investing huge sums of money in Asia, Africa and South America, only to take the profits out with no concern for the social betterment of the countries, and say: "This is not just." It will look at our alliance with the landed gentry of Latin America and say: "This is not just." The Western arrogance of feeling that it has everything to teach others and nothing to learn from them is not just. A true revolution of values will lay hands on the world order and say of war: "This way of settling differences is not just." This business of burning human beings with napalm, of filling our nation's homes with orphans and widows, of injecting poisonous drugs of hate into the veins of peoples normally humane, of sending men home from dark and bloody battlefields physically handicapped and psychologically deranged, cannot be reconciled with wisdom, justice, and love. A nation that continues year after year to spend more money on military defense than on programs of social uplift is approaching spiritual death.

America, the richest and most powerful nation in the world, can well lead the way in this revolution of values. There is nothing, except a tragic death wish, to prevent us from re-ordering our priorities, so that the pursuit of peace will take precedence over the pursuit of war. There is nothing to keep us from molding a recalcitrant status-quo with bruised hands until we have fashioned it into a brotherhood.

This kind of positive revolution of values is our best defense against Communism. War is not the answer. Communism will never be defeated by the use of atomic bombs or nuclear weapons. Let us not join those who shout war and through their misguided passions urge the United States to relinquish its participation in the United Nations. These are days which demand wise restraint and calm reasonableness. We must not call everyone a Communist or an appeaser who advocates the seating of Red China in the United Nations and who recognizes that hate and hysteria are not the final answers to the problem of these turbulent days. We must not engage in a negative anti-Communism, but rather in a positive thrust for democracy, realizing that our greatest defense against Communism is to take offensive action in behalf of justice. We must with positive action seek to remove those conditions of poverty, insecurity and injustice which are the fertile soil in which the seed of Communism grows and develops.

These are revolutionary times. All over the globe men are revolting against old systems of exploitation and oppression and out of the wombs of a frail world new systems of justice and equality are being born. The shirtless and barefoot people of the land are rising up as never before. "The people who sat in darkness have seen a great light." We in the West must support

these revolutions. It is a sad fact that, because of comfort, com-
placency, a morbid fear of Communism, and our proneness to
adjust to injustice, the Western nations that initiated so much of
the revolutionary spirit of the modern world have now become
the arch anti-revolutionaries. This has driven many to feel that
only Marxism has the revolutionary spirit. Therefore, Communism is a judgment against our failure to make democracy real
and follow through on the revolutions that we initiated. Our
only hope today lies in our ability to recapture the revolutionary
spirit and go out into a sometimes hostile world declaring eternal
hostility to poverty, racism, and militarism. With this powerful
commitment we shall boldly challenge the status-quo and unjust
mores and thereby speed the day when "every valley shall be exalted, and every mountain and hill shall be made low, and the
crooked shall be made straight and the rough places plain."

A genuine revolution of values means in the final analysis
that our loyalties must become ecumenical rather than sectional.
Every nation must now develop an overriding loyalty to mankind as a whole in order to preserve the best in their individual
societies.

This call for a world-wide fellowship that lifts neighborly concern beyond one's tribe, race, class and nation is in reality a call
for an all-embracing and unconditional love for all men. This oft
misunderstood and misinterpreted concept—so readily dismissed
by the Nietzsches of the world as a weak and cowardly force—
has now become an absolute necessity for the survival of man.
When I speak of love I am not speaking of some sentimental and
weak response. I am speaking of that force which all of the great
religions have seen as the supreme unifying principle of life. Love
is somehow the key that unlocks the door which leads to ultimate reality. This Hindu-Moslem-Christian-Jewish-Buddhist belief about ultimate reality is beautifully summed up in the first
epistle of Saint John:

Let us love one another; for love is God and everyone that
loveth is born of God and knoweth God. He that loveth

not knoweth not God; for God is love. If we love one another, God dwelleth in us, and his love is perfected in us.

Let us hope that this spirit will become the order of the day.
We can no longer afford to worship the God of hate or bow before
the altar of retaliation. The oceans of history are made turbulent by the ever-rising tides of hate. History is cluttered with the
wreckage of nations and individuals that pursued this self-defeating path of hate. As Arnold Toynbee says: "Love is the ultimate
force that makes for the saving choice of life and good against
the damning choice of death and evil. Therefore the first hope in
our inventory must be the hope that love is going to have the last
word."

We are now faced with the fact that tomorrow is today. We are
confronted with the fierce urgency of now. In this unfolding conundrum of life and history there is such a thing as being too late.
Procrastination is still the thief of time. Life often leaves us standing bare, naked and dejected with a lost opportunity. The "tide
in the affairs of men" does not remain at the flood; it ebbs. We
may cry out desperately for time to pause in her passage, but time
is deaf to every plea and rushes on. Over the bleached bones and
jumbled residue of numerous civilizations are written the pathetic
words: "Too late." There is an invisible book of life that faithfully
records our vigilance or our neglect. "The moving finger writes,
and having written moves on." We still have a choice today: nonviolent co-existence or violent co-annihilation.

We must move past indecision to action. We must find new
ways to speak for peace in Vietnam and justice throughout the developing world—a world that borders on our doors. If we do not
act we shall surely be dragged down the long dark and shameful
corridors of time reserved for those who possess power without
compassion, might without morality, and strength without sight.

Now let us begin. Now let us re-dedicate ourselves to the long
and bitter—but beautiful—struggle for a new world. This is the
calling of the sons of God, and our brothers wait eagerly for our
response. Shall we say the odds are too great? Shall we tell them

the struggle is too hard? Will our message be that the forces of American life militate against their arrival as full men, and we send our deepest regrets? Or will there be another message, of longing, of hope, of solidarity with their yearnings, of commitment to their cause, whatever the cost? The choice is ours, and though we might prefer it otherwise we *must* choose in this crucial moment of human history.

"The Middle East Question"

Statement by Martin Luther King, Jr., and the Southern Christian Leadership Conference (SCLC)

CHICAGO, SEPTEMBER 1967

———◇◇◇———

Serious distortions by the press have created an impression that SCLC was part of a group at the Chicago Conference of New Politics which introduced a resolution condemning Israel and unqualifiedly endorsing all the policies of the Arab powers. The facts are as follows:

1. The staff members of SCLC who attended the conference (not as official delegates) were the most vigorous and articulate opponents of the simplistic resolution on the Middle East question. As a result of this opposition the Black caucus modified its stand and the convention voted to eliminate references to Zionism and referred to the executive board the matter of final wording. This change was the direct result of the spirited opposition on the floor by Hosea Williams, Southern Director of SCLC.

2. SCLC and Dr. King have repeatedly stated that the Middle East problem embodies the related questions of security and development. *Israel's right to exist as a state in security is incontestable. At the same time the great powers have the obligation to recognize that the Arab world is in a state of imposed poverty and backwardness that must threaten peace and harmony.* Until a concerted and democratic program of assistance is affected, tensions cannot be relieved. Neither Israel nor its neighbors can live in peace without an underlying basis of economic and social development.

   At the heart of the problem are oil interests. As the American Jewish Congress has stated "American policies in the Middle East have been motivated in no small measure by the desire to protect the $2,500,000,000 stake which U.S. oil companies have invested in the area." Some Arab feudal rulers are no less concerned for oil wealth and neglect the plight of their own peoples. The solution will have to be found in statesmanship by Israel and progressive Arab forces who in concert with the great powers recognize that fair and peaceful solutions are the concern of all of humanity and must be found.

Neither military measures nor a stubborn effort to reverse history can provide a permanent solution for peoples who need and deserve both development and security.

3. SCLC and Dr. King have expressly, frequently and vigorously denounced anti-Semitism and will continue to do so. It is not only that anti-Semitism is immoral—though that alone is enough. It is used to divide Negro and Jew, who have effectively collaborated in the struggle for justice. It injures Negroes because it upholds the doctrine of racism which they have the greatest stake in destroying. The individual Jew or gentile who may be an exploiter acts out of his greed as an individual, not his religious precepts—just as a criminal—Negro or white—is expressing his anti-social tendencies—not the ethical values of his race.

SCLC will continue tirelessly to denounce racism, whether its form is white supremacy or anti-Semitism.

"War and the World House"

Statement by Martin Luther King, Jr.

From *Where Do We Go from Here:*
Chaos or Community?

1967

A final problem that mankind must solve in order to survive in the world house that we have inherited is finding an alternative to war and human destruction. Recent events have vividly reminded us that nations are not reducing but rather increasing their arsenals of weapons of mass destruction. The best brains in the highly developed nations of the world are devoted to military technology. The proliferation of nuclear weapons has not been halted, in spite of the limited-test-ban treaty.

In this day of man's highest technical achievement, in this day of dazzling discovery, of novel opportunities, loftier dignities and fuller freedoms for all, there is no excuse for the kind of blind craving for power and resources that provoked the wars of previous generations. There is no need to fight for food and land. Science has provided us with adequate means of survival and transportation, which make it possible to enjoy the fullness of this great earth. The question now is, do we have the morality and courage required to live together as brothers and not be afraid?

One of the most persistent ambiguities we face is that everybody talks about peace as a goal, but among the wielders of power peace is practically nobody's business. Many men cry "Peace! Peace!" but they refuse to do the things that make for peace.

The large power blocs talk passionately of pursuing peace while expanding defense budgets that already bulge, enlarging already awesome armies and devising ever more devastating weapons. Call the roll of those who sing the glad tidings of peace and one's ears will be surprised by the responding sounds. The heads of all the nations issue clarion calls for peace, yet they come to the peace table accompanied by bands of brigands each bearing unsheathed swords.

The stages of history are replete with the chants and choruses of the conquerors of old who came killing in pursuit of peace. Alexander, Genghis Khan, Julius Caesar, Charlemagne and Napoleon were akin in seeking a peaceful world order, a world fashioned after their selfish conceptions of an ideal existence. Each sought a world at peace which would personify his egotistic dreams. Even within the life span of most of us, another megalomaniac strode across the world stage. He sent his blitzkrieg-bent legions blazing across Europe, bringing havoc and holocaust in his wake. There is grave irony in the fact that Hitler could come forth, following nakedly aggressive expansionist theories, and do it all in the name of peace.

So when in this day I see the leaders of nations again talking peace while preparing for war, I take fearful pause. When I see our country today intervening in what is basically a civil war, mutilating hundreds of thousands of Vietnamese children with napalm, burning villages and rice fields at random, painting the valleys of that small Asian country red with human blood, leaving broken bodies in countless ditches and sending home half-men, mutilated mentally and physically; when I see the unwillingness of our government to create the atmosphere for a negotiated settlement of this awful conflict by halting bombings in the North and agreeing unequivocally to talk with the Vietcong—and all this in the name of pursuing the goal of peace—I tremble for our world. I do so not only from dire recall of the nightmares wreaked in the wars of yesterday, but also from dreadful realization of today's possible nuclear destructiveness and tomorrow's even more calamitous prospects.

Before it is too late, we must narrow the gaping chasm between our proclamations of peace and our lowly deeds which precipitate and perpetuate war. We are called upon to look up from the quagmire of military programs and defense commitments and read the warnings on history's signposts.

One day we must come to see that peace is not merely a distant goal that we seek but a means by which we arrive at that goal. We must pursue peaceful ends through peaceful means. How much longer must we play at deadly war games before we heed the plaintive pleas of the unnumbered dead and maimed of past wars?

President John F. Kennedy said on one occasion, "Mankind must put an end to war or war will put an end to mankind." Wisdom born of experience should tell us that war is obsolete. There may have been a time when war served as a negative good by preventing the spread and growth of an evil force, but the destructive power of modern weapons eliminates even the possibility that war may serve any good at all. If we assume that life is worth living and that man has a right to survive, then we must find an alternative to war. In a day when vehicles hurtle through outer space and guided ballistic missiles carve highways of death through the stratosphere, no nation can claim victory in war. A so-called limited war will leave little more than a calamitous legacy of human suffering, political turmoil and spiritual disillusionment. A world war will leave only smoldering ashes as mute testimony of a human race whose folly led inexorably to ultimate death. If modern man continues to flirt unhesitatingly with war, he will transform his earthly habitat into an inferno such as even the mind of Dante could not imagine.

Therefore I suggest that the philosophy and strategy of nonviolence become immediately a subject for study and for serious experimentation in every field of human conflict, by no means excluding the relations between nations. It is, after all, nation-states which make war, which have produced the weapons that threaten the survival of mankind and which are both genocidal and suicidal in character.

We have ancient habits to deal with, vast structures of power, indescribably complicated problems to solve. But unless we abdicate our humanity altogether and succumb to fear and impotence in the presence of the weapons we have ourselves created, it is as possible and as urgent to put an end to war and violence between nations as it is to put an end to poverty and racial injustice.

The United Nations is a gesture in the direction of nonviolence on a world scale. There, at least, states that oppose one another have sought to do so with words instead of with weapons. But true nonviolence is more than the absence of violence. It is the persistent and determined application of peaceable power to offenses against the community—in this case the world community. As the United Nations moves ahead with the giant tasks confronting it, I would hope that it would earnestly examine the uses of nonviolent direct action.

I do not minimize the complexity of the problems that need to be faced in achieving disarmament and peace. But I am convinced that we shall not have the will, the courage and the insight to deal with such matters unless in this field we are prepared to undergo a mental and spiritual reevaluation, a change of focus which will enable us to see that the things that seem most real and powerful are indeed now unreal and have come under sentence of death. We need to make a supreme effort to generate the readiness, indeed the eagerness, to enter into the new world which is now possible, "the city which hath foundation, whose Building and Maker is God."

It is not enough to say, "We must not wage war." It is necessary to love peace and sacrifice for it. We must concentrate not merely on the eradication of war but on the affirmation of peace. A fascinating story about Ulysses and the Sirens is preserved for us in Greek literature. The Sirens had the ability to sing so sweetly that sailors could not resist steering toward their island. Many ships were lured upon the rocks, and men forgot home, duty and honor as they flung themselves into the sea to be embraced by arms that drew them down to death. Ulysses, determined not to succumb to the Sirens, first decided to tie himself tightly to the mast of his boat and his crew stuffed their ears with wax. But finally he and his crew learned a better way to save themselves: They took on board the beautiful singer Orpheus, whose melodies were sweeter than the music of the Sirens. When Orpheus sang, who would bother to listen to the Sirens?

So we must see that peace represents a sweeter music, a cosmic melody that is far superior to the discords of war. Somehow we must transform the dynamics of the world power struggle from the nuclear arms race, which no one can win, to a creative contest to harness man's genius for the purpose of making peace and prosperity a reality for all the nations of the world. In short, we must shift the arms race into a "peace race." If we have the will and determination to mount such a peace offensive, we will unlock hitherto tightly sealed doors of hope and bring new light into the dark chambers of pessimism.

PART VI

Toward a Positive Pluralism:
Interfaith Dialogue and
Global Community

*Ever since the dawn of the Christian era, Christians have
considered it a serious part of their basic responsibility to
carry the gospel of Jesus Christ into all the world and to
every creature. This is one of the things that distinguishes
Christianity from the other great religions of the world.
Most of the other great religions have had profound
admiration for their founders, but they do not consider
it a serious part of their responsibility to carry the message
of their founders into all the world.*

— "Redirecting Our Missionary Zeal," a handwritten
outline, Montgomery, Alabama, January 22, 1956

Introduction

M artin Luther King, Jr., had a respect for global religious
pluralism that is seldom mentioned even in the most care-
ful and extensive studies of his life, thought, and activities. He
ultimately came to the conclusion that no one religion has a monopoly on truth and wisdom, and he often alluded to the timeless
values shared by Christianity, Judaism, Islam, Hinduism, Buddhism, and other "great world religions." Even as he functioned
from a Judeo-Christian base, King believed and said repeatedly
that the various faith traditions were essentially united in their beliefs about ultimate reality—and in their conceptions of love "as
the supreme unifying principle of life." Thus, King could speak
of a fundamental congruence between his own Christian beliefs
and values and those held and practiced by Jews, Muslims, Hindus, Buddhists, and representatives of other religions. To be sure,
King's "world house" or beloved community ideal amounted to
a sort of overarching telos that embraced all religions as valid
pointers to God.

Strangely enough, King was also the product of a nation in
which most people of faith professed to be Christians, especially
evangelical and fundamentalist types, and the vast majority did
not share his appreciation of and respect for other world religions.
The view that Christianity was the highest revelation of God and
the only route to salvation was widely embraced, even by the so-
called Negro churches, which afforded the de facto platform for
King's civil rights campaigns. This idea of the exclusivity of salvation based on the Christian faith was the motivation behind the
many physical and material resources that the American churches
devoted to Christian missions in Africa, Asia, and other parts of
the globe. King struggled with, and in time categorically rejected,
this sort of religious worldview but understood that, under the
circumstances, he had too much to lose by consistently putting
his thoughts on religious pluralism on public display. Rejecting

the sense of missionary urgency and compassion held by most Christians in the United States, King, in a statement in the *Chicago Defender* of May 29–June 4, 1965, argued that "Christianity should be a crusade not against infidels but against injustice."

Several statements, two letters, and an article are found in part VI of *"In a Single Garment of Destiny."* The significance of these documents is evident on three levels. First, they reveal King's own intellectual pilgrimage and growth around the question of religious pluralism. Second, they explain King's powerful case for a rethinking and recasting of traditional ways of thinking about religion, and especially religious diversity. Finally, King's idea of interfaith or pan-religious dialogue as both conversation and cooperative, concrete action in the interest of justice, peace, reconciliation, and community is clearly revealed.

"Christianity and African Religions," which appeared in the September 1958 issue of *Ebony*, is the very first document included here. It was written when King was a very young pastor and in the early stage of his civil rights leadership in Montgomery, Alabama. For a year, King had been writing an advice column in *Ebony*, a black-owned monthly magazine, answering a range of questions put to him by readers on race relations, religion, and matters of personal ethics. King wrote the statement "Christianity and African Religions" in response to a question about whether or not Christianity was more valid than the tribal religions of his African ancestors. While acknowledging God's revelation in all religions, King declared that Christianity embodied "the highest revelation of God" and was therefore more "valid" than African tribal religions. King's view that God was revealed completely and uniquely in Jesus Christ never really changed, but in future statements he was less prone to assert the superiority of Christianity over other religions, especially when communicating with persons who adhered to religions other than his own. "Christianity and African Religions" is made available in this volume because it reveals a King who, despite his open-mindedness, had not broken completely with the dominant American attitude toward so-called non-Christian religions. It was also a King who had not yet had serious and extensive encounters with other world religions and their leaders.

"I Have Never Been a Religious Bigot" is the title given to a letter King wrote to Mr. M. Bernard Resnikoff on September 17, 1961. This document appears here because it offers a perspective on religious pluralism that is missing in "Christianity and African Religions," the aforementioned document, especially in its assault on the failures of Western Christianity and its suggestion that religions are equally valid as expressions of divine revelation and truth. King came increasingly to recognize the ignorance and misunderstanding with which most Americans greeted religious pluralism, and was open to a new way of thinking on the issue. Also, King detected in time that the lack of knowledge of and appreciation for world religions as a whole were too often part of the hidden dynamics in international relations, and that this had to change if genuine world peace and community were to be actualized. King ultimately determined that religious diversity was healthy and had to be affirmed and celebrated, and he attributed religious bigotry and intolerance largely to the Christian Church's failure to witness to a gospel that unites people across religious boundaries. In King's estimation, much-needed church renewal could not occur without a positive and constructive encounter with all the great world religions.

"A Narrow Sectarianism That Causes Me Real Concern" is the title attached to King's letter to Dr. Harold E. Fey, the editor of the *Christian Century*, the flagship magazine of mainline Protestantism, dated June 23, 1962. Apparently, King's involvement with the recently formed Gandhi Society for Human Rights (GSHR), "a crucible for new ideas and nonviolent direct action," was being questioned in some Christian circles in the United States, and mainly by Protestant leaders like Fey and John Morris of the Episcopal Society for Cultural and Racial Unity (ESCRU). King wrote the letter to Dr. Fey to clarify the role of the GSHR, and to dismiss the suggestion that he was breaking with Christianity and joining a new sect.

Obviously, King used the opportunity once again to denounce

religious bigotry and intolerance, and to repeat his claim that all religions are sources of truth and God's revelation. He also mentioned Mohandas K. Gandhi, the Hindu who led Indian people in their struggle for independence from British colonial domination, to illustrate his point that God had a witness in every religion. But King also reaffirmed his conviction that God's revelation through Christ is the highest revelation, a point not made in the aforementioned letter to M. Bernard Resnikoff. Apparently, the fact that Resnikoff was Jewish and Fey Christian essentially dictated the nature of King's response to each.

"All the Great Religions of the World" is included here because it is probably King's most extensive and profound statement on how Christianity, Judaism, Islam, Buddhism, and Hinduism might be effective in promoting peace and goodwill. King produced this statement for *Redbook Magazine* on November 5, 1964. While noting how religion had been used historically to feed tendencies toward violence and domination, King evidently thought that "all the great religions of the world" could be a positive influence in the quest for world peace and community, especially if they chose to be true to their creeds. This is the central point of the statement. Thus, King called for a united faith witness against all forms of violence and injustice, and brought an interfaith or pan-religious character to his civil and human rights activities. He intersected Protestants, Catholics, and Jews in his civil rights campaigns in the American South, and, as indicated in part II of this volume, united with people of virtually every faith tradition in promoting appeals, declarations, and petitions in the interest of justice, human dignity, and peace. Here King was practically applying his belief that the beloved community must be lived out in an ecumenical and pan-religious fellowship of love and cooperative action. Undoubtedly, he understood that there is a universal path to God's Kingdom that intersects with people of all faith claims. This was part of his creative interpretation of the Kingdom of God motif.

King wrote "My Jewish Brother!" for the February 26, 1966, issue of the *New York Amsterdam News*, a black-owned newspaper. This article is included in part VI because it reflected King's sense of the evils of anti-Semitism. Here King denounced anti-Semitism as a great social evil, and affirmed the pressing and continuing need for Jewish allies in the struggle for a better nation and world. Recalling the biblical Hebrew prophets, who attacked social evils and proclaimed the importance of the ethical life, King went on to assert that more Hebrew prophets were needed in his time to meet the challenges of hatred, intolerance, and war. King referred to the global significance of Judaism on numerous occasions, especially when speaking to Jewish groups and interfaith conferences. He actually learned from his study of all the great religions, and forged from this a core of philosophy and methods that was useful in his assault on a multitude of social evils.

Convinced that more truth inheres in all the world religions combined than in any one religion alone, and that all religions embody rich resources and opportunities for learning, King became a staunch advocate for interfaith or pan-religious dialogue. But he had in mind not merely academic models of conversation between representatives of the different faith traditions but also cooperative social activism for the benefit of humanity as a whole. This explains the decision to include "Buddhists and Martyrs of the Civil Rights Movement," King's joint statement with the Buddhist monk Thich Nhat Hanh, in part VI. The statement, which is the last document in this volume, affirmed that black civil rights workers and Vietnamese peace activists were engaged in a common struggle for freedom, equality, and peaceful coexistence. Moreover, it declared that the "real enemies" of humanity everywhere were not people themselves but the evil and misguided spirit that lurked in human hearts and minds. This joint statement by King and Hanh is one of the most important documents in this volume, especially since it speaks to the shared vision, hopes, and dreams of two leaders of vastly different faith traditions. Interestingly enough, King, who received the Nobel Peace Prize in 1964, recommended Hanh for the same honor in 1967.

Obviously, King's connections and collaborative social justice efforts with representatives of various world religions were unique for a Christian clergyman in his time. In 1967, King even joined Muhammad Ali, the black Muslim, in putting out a joint statement in opposition to systems of oppression. King also spoke, sang, prayed, and marched with Jewish rabbis like Abraham J. Heschel and Everett Gendler, and learned timeless truths and models of social activism from Mohandas K. Gandhi. A reciprocity and deep spiritual kinship united King with figures like Hanh, Ali, Heschel, Gendler and Gandhi, and their encounters with each other were indicative of how certain kinds of faith claims and ethical values might move across different religious traditions. Their shared values intersected with a global human rights agenda and inspired a collective sense of social responsibility.

The world has become ever more globalized since King's death in 1968, and we are increasingly confronted with and challenged by a diversity of religious beliefs and practices. People worldwide are encountering on a daily basis someone unlike themselves, religiously and culturally, but all too few seem willing to embrace and accept the historical and social reality of the many religions. Disturbing patterns of Islamophobia are emerging throughout parts of the United States and Europe today, and cycles of violence are erupting between Hindus and Christians in India, Muslims and Christians in Egypt, Jews and Muslims in the Middle East, and Muslim factions throughout the Arab world. In such a global climate, King's sense of the role that all the major religions can play in forging a richer vision of humanity's universality in an interdependent and interrelated world needs to be seriously studied. We might also benefit from King's understanding of how the different religions might contribute to responsible engagement with contemporary societal and global problems and challenges.

The documents in part VI of "In a Single Garment of Destiny," much like those in parts I–V, expose the reader to the thinking, vision, and mission of the global Martin Luther King, Jr. They also help explain why King continues to elicit widespread interest from people on the most diverse points of the religious and ideological spectrum.

"Christianity and African Religions"

Excerpted Statement by Martin Luther King, Jr.

Ebony

SEPTEMBER 1958

——◇✕◇——

QUESTION: *Is Christianity, as a religion, more valid than the tribal religions practiced at one time by Africans?*

ANSWER: I believe that God reveals Himself in all religions. Wherever we find truth we find the revelation of God, and there is some element of truth in all religions. This does not mean, however, that God reveals Himself equally in all religions. Christianity is an expression of the highest revelation of God. It is the synthesis of the best in all religions. In this sense Christianity is more valid than the tribal religions practiced by our African ancestors. This does not mean that these tribal religions are totally devoid of truth. It simply means that Christianity, while flowing through the stream of history, has incorporated the truths of all other religions and brought them together into a meaningful and coherent system. Moreover, at the center of Christianity stands the Christ who is now and ever shall be the highest revelation of God. He, more than any other person that has ever lived in history, reveals the true nature of God. Through his life, death, and resurrection the power of eternity broke forth into time.

"I Have Never Been a Religious Bigot"

Letter from Martin Luther King, Jr., to Mr. M. Bernard Resnikoff

FAIRLAWN, NEW JERSEY, SEPTEMBER 17, 1961

Mr. M. Bernard Resnikoff
3601 Lenox Drive
Fairlawn, New Jersey

Dear Mr. Resnikoff:

Thank you for your letter of August 18. Absence from the city has delayed my reply.

I regret so much that you misinterpreted a statement that I made in Miami, Florida some weeks ago. When I referred to America becoming a Christian nation, I was not referring to Christianity as an organized institutional religion. I was referring more to the principles of Christ, which I think are sound and valid for any nation and civilization. I have never been a victim of religious bigotry. I have never condemned any of the great religions of the world, for it is my sincere conviction that no religion has a monopoly on truth and that God has revealed Himself in all of the religions of mankind. So let me assure you that when I speak of America rising to the heights of a Democratic and Christian nation, I am referring to the need of rising to the heights of noble ethical and moral principles. I am sure that you are aware of the fact that many people, Christians and non-Christians, theists and humanists, have found within the Sermon on the Mount and other insights of Jesus Christ, great ethical principles that they can adhere to even though they would not accept institutionalized Christianity.

I am very sorry that you are so offended by the word Christian. Maybe it is due to the fact that we Christians have not always been Christian in our dealing with people of other religions, and sometimes in our dealings with people of our own religion.

Very sincerely yours,

Martin Luther King, Jr.

"A Narrow Sectarianism That
Causes Me Real Concern"

Letter from Martin Luther King, Jr., to
Dr. Harold E. Fey, editor of *The Christian Century*

JUNE 23, 1962

———∞◇∞———

Dear Dr. Fey:

It is very seldom that I pause to answer criticisms that are directed toward me and my work. If I stopped to answer all of the criticisms that come across my desk, I would find little time to do anything else and my office staff would be almost completely involved in this task. However, the editorial which appeared in *The Christian Century* and the statement released by The Rev. John Morris, of the Episcopal Society for Cultural and Racial Unity, reveal such a blatant misunderstanding of the new Gandhi Society for Human Rights that I feel compelled to answer it.

First, I should give you some idea of the circumstances that led to the formation of the Gandhi Society. Several months ago I met with a group of distinguished lawyers in New York and solicited their support in the libel cases that several Alabama officials had brought against four ministers of the Southern Christian Leadership Conference. These lawyers were so outraged at this tragic misuse of the judicial process that they immediately formed a lawyer's committee to give legal and financial assistance to these victims of injustice. When one realizes that the SCLC has already spent over $40,000.00 on the libel cases, it is not too difficult to see what a tremendous lift it was to me to get the support of these lawyers.

As these men came closer and closer to the struggle, they came to a realization of the overwhelming financial burden that we were facing in the non-violent movement. They saw how our all-too-limited financial resources were constantly drained by the legal maneuvering and vicious attacks of those who opposed our efforts. As a result of this, many felt that a tax exempt fund should be set up through which large scale financial support could be channelized for the non-violent movement. Along with this, the idea emerged that this fund could also serve as a medium through which educational material on non-violence could be disseminated on a broad scale and support for voter education on a more partisan basis could be developed. Out of this interplay of ideas and concerns the Gandhi Society had its birth. It is not a new civil rights organization such as NAACP, Urban League, SCLC or CORE. It is rather an educational fund or foundation which was established to serve as a crucible for new ideas and non-violent direct action, and to provide support for the movement to increase the number of Negro registered voters, and to provide legal aid to those leaders and individuals who are regularly attacked because of their involvement in the non-violent movement.

It is clear from the foregoing that the founders of the Gandhi Society had not the slightest desire to set up an organization that would displace the church or repudiate the Christian gospel. This question never came up, and I am sure that no one in the group considered this new thrust as a substitute for the social action program of the Christian church.

At this point, I think I should state my personal convictions on the issue. Both you and Mr. Morris imply in your statements that I am now forsaking the Christian church in order to turn to a new kind of American sectarianism. You seem to have the idea that the Gandhi Society will replace the Southern Christian Leadership Conference. This is implied in your statement that "They are likely to be disappointed with the results of this organizational re-shuffling and re-naming." Suffice it to say that the SCLC, of which I am president, is more alive than ever before. We have some seventy-five affiliate organizations covering every Southern State. We work mainly through the churches to achieve citizenship rights for Negroes and to instill the philosophy of Christian non-violence. There is not the slightest idea of giving up this approach. My connection with SCLC is that of Executive President and most of my time and energy are given to the implementation of this program. The Gandhi Society has no organic or structural connection with SCLC. My only connection with the Society is that of Honorary Chairman. How anyone could interpret my relation with the Gandhi Society as a turn away from the church is a real mystery to me. As far as my Christology goes, I believe as firmly now as ever that God revealed himself uniquely and completely through Jesus Christ. Like Thomas of old, I, too, can affirm in the presence of Christ, "My Lord, and my God." I believe with every Christian in the Lordship of Jesus Christ and I am more convinced than ever before that we will only find the solution to the problems of the world through Christ and his way.

One's commitment to Jesus Christ as Lord and Savior, however, should not mean that one cannot be inspired by another great personality that enters the stage of history. I must confess that I saw in your statement and that of Mr. Morris a narrow sectarianism and a degree of religious intolerance that cause me real concern. While I firmly believe that God reveals himself more completely and uniquely in Christianity than any other religion, I cannot make myself believe that God did not reveal himself in other religions. I believe that in some marvelous way, God worked through Gandhi, and the spirit of Jesus Christ saturated his life. It is ironic, yet inescapably true that the greatest Christian of the modern world was a man who never embraced Christianity. This is not an indictment on Christ but a tribute to Him—a tribute to his universality and His Lordship. When I think of Gandhi, I think of the Master's way in the words of the fourth gospel: "I have other sheep that are not of this fold." This is not to make of Gandhi a new Jesus Christ—this he can never be. It is fallacious to think of the Gandhi Society as an attempt to deify Gandhi or establish a cult around his name. It seems only natural for this new foundation to take the name of Gandhi since he, more than anyone in the modern world, lifted the method of non-violence to a powerful level of socio-political action. To say that a Society formed with the name of Gandhi to give aid to those engaged in the non-violent struggle for justice is the establishment of a new cult, is as illogical as saying that a foundation established in the name of Albert Schweitzer or Tom Dooley to aid in medical care for Asian and African people is the development of a new cult.

To sum up all that I have said: you have been misinformed on at least two points. (1) You have the impression that the Gandhi Society is a new civil rights organization. This, it is not. It is an educational fund. (2) You have the impression that the Gandhi Society is made up of Christian leaders who have deserted Christ and the church. Nothing could be further from the truth. The Christian leaders on the Board of the Gandhi Society are more involved in making the gospel relevant in this period of social change than ever before.

I must say in conclusion that I was somewhat shocked to discover that you and Mr. Morris would so vehemently attack the Gandhi Society without first getting a statement from me concerning its nature and purpose. Certainly I do not wish to imply that my views and my work should not be criticized when necessary. But for one to criticize without knowing all of the facts is both unjust and unfair. Just a telephone call or a letter could have cleared up most of your misconceptions. Naturally I would not expect most journalists to speak to me to clarify the facts before releasing a statement, but it is a Christian courtesy that I would expect from a dedicated Priest who is an ally in the struggle and from a responsible periodical that does not hesitate to use my name as an Editor-at-Large. I have come to see over the past few years that most misunderstandings in the world develop because of a lack of communication—the tragic tendency to live in monologue rather than dialogue. I am extremely sorry that your editorial and the statement of Mr. Morris will spread so many unfortunate misconceptions about the Gandhi Society and will cause many Christian leaders to look upon it with strange suspicion and doubt my own commitment to Christ and the church. It may even cause some to withhold financial support—and this can be a tragedy when one considers the burden and the strain that all of us face in seeking to raise funds for the civil rights struggle.

I am sure that, as in the past, when our humble efforts have been misinterpreted, and temporary setbacks have been our fate, we will be sustained by Him whose grace and power will keep us from falling.

Very sincerely yours,

Martin Luther King, Jr.

P. S. I am not writing this letter for publication.

"All the Great Religions of the World"

Statement by Martin Luther King, Jr.

Prepared for *Redbook Magazine*

NOVEMBER 5, 1964

—◇◇◇—

*What evidence is there that religion has ever been, or in the
future could be, effective in promoting peace and goodwill
among men? Or do you feel that peace depends primarily
on new social and political institutions?*

MARTIN LUTHER KING, JR.: Religion at its best has always sought
to promote peace and good will among men. This is true of all
of the great religions of the world. In their ethical systems, we
find the love ethic standing at the center. This is true of Judaism, this is true of Christianity, this is true of Islam, of Hinduism and Buddhism, and if we go right through all the great
religions of the world we find this central message of love and this
idea of the need for peace, the need for understanding and the
need for good will among men. Now the problem has been that
these noble creeds and ethical insights of the great religions have
not been followed by the adherents of the particular religions,
and we must face the shameful fact that all too many religious
people have been religious in their creeds but not enough in their
deeds. I have felt all along that if religion—and this includes all
religions—would take a real stand against war and go all-out for
peace and brotherhood, then we would be further along the way
in making these into reality. I think the two are tied together. I
don't think there can be peace without brotherhood, and I don't
think you can have brotherhood without peace. To put it another
way, I don't think there can be justice without peace, and I don't
think there can be peace without justice. If religious institutions
had really been true to their creeds all along, to the demand for

justice, the demand for peace, then we would have peace and justice. Now even though there has been a great deal of negligence and even though the religions of the world have not done enough to inspire their followers to work passionately and unrelentingly for peace, I think that in the present and the future religion *can* play a great role. If brotherhood is to become a reality, religion must somehow get into the thick of the battle for peace and reaffirm the fact that, as the Old Testament says, men must beat their swords into plowshares and their spears into pruning hooks, and nations must not rise up against nations; neither must they study war any more. If we are to have a just and lasting peace, religion will have to do more to influence the minds of men and women and be true to their ethical insights. Now I don't say that political institutions don't have a great role to play, and I'm not unmindful of the fact that there are millions of people under political systems that would deny any claim to religion as we know it because they are basically atheistic systems. Still I don't want to go so far as to say that in these systems there can't be a longing for peace. I firmly believe that religion or even God is that which concerns man *ultimately*. When we deal with the ultimate concerns, we are dealing with individuals who whether they know it or not have some form of religion. So I think that even in those situations there can be a longing for peace. But I am sure that if the religions of the world are to bring about the peace that I am talking about and create the climate for it, they've got to rise to the level of not fighting among themselves. Some of the most tragic wars in the world have been religious wars. There is a need for individual religions to realize that God has revealed Himself to all religions and there is some truth in all. And no religion can permit itself to be so arrogant that it fails to see that God has not left Himself without a witness, even though it may be in another religion.

"My Jewish Brother!"

Article by Martin Luther King, Jr.

New York Amsterdam News

NEW YORK, NEW YORK, FEBRUARY 26, 1966

———◇◇◇———

Recently, I was saddened—as I am sure many other Americans were—to read that one of the leaders of a fine and militant civil rights group had made an anti-Semitic remark.

In the heat of a controversy over school desegregation, this individual, who is a Negro, shouted to his audience, which included a number of Jewish people, a statement to the effect that Hitler had not killed enough Jews.

Actually, I do not view this horrible outburst as anti-Jewish. I see it as anti-man and anti-God. It would be a statement to harshly condemn, coming from anyone. It is singularly despicable, coming from the lips of a black man.

For, black people, who have been torturously burned in the crucible of hatred for centuries, should have become so purified of hate in those scorching flames as to be instinctively intolerant of intolerance. In the struggle for human rights, as well as in the struggle for the upward march of our civilization, we have deep need for the partnership, fellowship and courage of our Jewish Brother. History will attest that the Hebrew prophets belong to all people.

For, it has been their concepts of justice and equality which have become ideals for all races and civilizations.

Today, we particularly need the Hebrew prophets because they taught that to love God was to love justice; that each human being has an inescapable obligation to denounce evil where he sees it and to defy a ruler who commands him to break the covenant.

The Hebrew prophets are needed today because decent people

must be imbued with the courage to speak the truth, to realize that silence may temporarily preserve status or security but that to live with a lie is a gross affront to God.

It is scarcely a secret that many congressmen, educators, clergymen and leaders of national affairs are gravely disturbed by our foreign policy.

A war in which children are incinerated by napalm, in which American soldiers die in mounting numbers while other American soldiers, according to press accounts, in unrestrained hatred shoot the wounded enemy as he lies upon the ground, is a war that mutilates the conscience. Yet, important leaders keep their silence.

I know this to be true because so many have confided in me that they shared my opinions, but not my willingness to state them in public.

The Hebrew prophets are needed today because we need their flaming courage. We need them because the thunder of their fearless voices is the only sound stronger than the blasts of bombs and the clamour of war hysteria.

The Hebrew prophets are needed today because Amos said, in words that echo across the centuries: "Let justice roll down like the waters and righteousness as a mighty stream." We need them because Micah said, in words lifted to cosmic proportions, "They shall beat their swords into plowshares and their spears into pruning hooks. Nation shall not lift up sword against nation. Neither shall they learn war anymore."

We need them because Isaiah said: "Yes, when ye make many prayers, I will not hear. Your hands are full of blood. Wash you. Make you clean. Put away the evil of your doings from before mine eyes. Cease to do evil."

I think the Hebrew prophets are among us today because, although there are many pulpits that are empty while ministers physically occupy them, there are others from which the passion for justice and compassion for man is still heard.

In the days to come, as the voices of sanity multiply, we will know that, across thousands of years of time, the prophet's message of truth and decency, brotherhood and peace, survives; that they are living in our time, to give hope to a tortured world that their promise of the Kingdom of God has not been lost to mankind.

"Buddhists and Martyrs of the Civil Rights Movement"

Joint Statement by
Martin Luther King, Jr.,
and Thich Nhat Hanh

International Committee of Conscience on Vietnam

NYACK, NEW YORK, 1966

———◇◇◇———

We believe that the Buddhists who have sacrificed themselves, like the martyrs of the civil rights movement, do not aim at the injury of the oppressors but only at changing their policies. The enemies of those struggling for freedom and democracy are not man. They are discrimination, dictatorship, greed, hatred and violence, which lie within the heart of man. These are the real enemies of man—not man himself.

We also believe that the struggles for equality and freedom in Birmingham, Selma and Chicago, as in Hue, Danang and Saigon, are aimed not at the domination of one people by another. They are aimed at self-determination, peaceful social change, and a better life for all human beings. And we believe that only in a world of peace can the work of construction, of building good societies everywhere, go forward.

A NOTE ON SOURCES

The documents in this volume can be found among the King Papers at the Martin Luther King, Jr., Center for Nonviolent Social Change in Atlanta, Georgia, but some may also be found in the King collections at Boston University and Morehouse College. Some were previously published in the six volumes of *The Papers of Martin Luther King, Jr.*, edited by Clayborne Carson et al. and published by the University of California Press.

Verification of the existence of all of the documents is provided through historical archives, published books and articles by and about Martin Luther King, Jr., and other documentary sources. A few of the documents were verified through the *New York Amsterdam News*, a New York–based black newspaper; the *Mennonite*; and *Ebony* magazine. Useful collections of sources include the papers of the American Committee on Africa and the American Negro Leadership Conference on Africa at the Amistad Research Center at Tulane University, as well as issues of the *New York Amsterdam News* at the Schomburg Center for Research in Black Culture in New York.

Some of King's speeches and statements were at times revised and presented in a number of different versions, and readers should be mindful of this as they study the materials in this volume. We have included what we believe to be the most extensive and accurate versions of the documents, in their original form and without major deletions and/or changes.

A number of letters, declarations, appeals, petitions, and other documents cosponsored and signed by King—addressing issues ranging from South African apartheid and the war in Vietnam to anti-Semitism—are not included in this volume. In the interest of space, we carefully selected documents that we think are most representative of King's positions on these and other issues of global significance. Listed below are the documents in the order in which they appear in this volume.

"The Vision of a World Made New." Speech before the Women's Convention Auxiliary of the National Baptist Convention, St. Louis, September 9, 1954. Speech taken from Clayborne Carson et al., eds., *The Papers of Martin Luther King, Jr., Volume VI: Advocate of the Social Gospel, September 1948–March 1963* (Berkeley: University of California Press, 2007), pages 181–184. Transcription and verification courtesy of the library and archives of the Martin Luther King, Jr., Center for Nonviolent Social Change, Atlanta.

"The World House." Statement taken from Martin Luther King, Jr., *Where Do We Go from Here: Chaos or Community?* (Boston: Beacon Press, 1968), pages 167–173.

"Revolution and Redemption." Closing address at the European Baptist Assembly, Amsterdam, August 16, 1964. Transcription and verification courtesy of the library and archives of the Martin Luther King, Jr., Center for Nonviolent Social Change, Atlanta.

"Declaration of Conscience." Joint statement against South African apartheid, with Bishop James A. Pike and Eleanor Roosevelt, New York, New York, July 1957. Transcription and verification courtesy of the library and archives of the Martin Luther King, Jr., Center for Nonviolent Social Change, Atlanta. Published version provided by the American Committee on Africa, New York City.

"Appeal for Action Against Apartheid." Joint statement against South African apartheid with the African National Congress leader Albert John Luthuli, New York, December 1962. Transcription and verification courtesy of the King Papers at the library and archives of the Martin Luther King, Jr., Center for Nonviolent Social Change, Atlanta. Published version provided by the American Committee on Africa, New York City.

"South African Independence." Speech against South African apartheid, London, December 7, 1964. Transcription and verification courtesy of the library and archives of the Martin Luther King, Jr., Center for Nonviolent Social Change, Atlanta.

"Let My People Go." Speech against South African apartheid, Hunter College, New York, December 10, 1965. Transcription and verification courtesy of the library and archives of the Martin Luther King, Jr., Center

for Nonviolent Social Change, Atlanta. Other titles used for this speech are "South African Benefit Speech" and "Call for an International Boycott on Apartheid South Africa."

"Invitation to South Africa." Letter to the South African Embassy, New Orleans, February 9, 1966. Transcription and verification courtesy of the library and archives of the Martin Luther King, Jr., Center for Nonviolent Social Change, Atlanta.

"On the World Taking a Stand on Rhodesia." Comment on racial apartheid in Rhodesia (Zimbabwe) and its similarities to the situation in South Africa, Paris, October 25, 1965. Transcription and verification courtesy of the library and archives of the Martin Luther King, Jr., Center for Nonviolent Social Change, Atlanta.

"Racism and the World House." Statement taken from Martin Luther King, Jr., *Where Do We Go from Here: Chaos or Community?* (Boston: Beacon Press, 1968), pages 173–176.

"Invitation to Ghana." Statement regarding an invitation to the independence ceremony in Ghana from Prime Minister Kwame Nkrumah, Montgomery, Alabama, March 1957. Transcription and verification courtesy of the library and archives of the Martin Luther King, Jr., Center for Nonviolent Social Change, Atlanta, and Special Collections, Mugar Memorial Library, Boston University, Boston.

"The Birth of a New Nation." Sermon concerning Ghanaian independence, Dexter Avenue Baptist Church, Montgomery, Alabama, April 7, 1957. Taken from *Call to Conscience: The Landmark Speeches of Dr. Martin Luther King, Jr.,* Clayborne Carson and Kris Shepard, eds. (New York: Grand Central Publishing, 2001).

"Introduction to Southwest Africa: The U.N.'s Stepchild." Statement on Southwest Africa, Montgomery, Alabama, October 1959. Taken from Clayborne Carson et al., eds., *The Papers of Martin Luther King, Jr., Volume V: Threshold of a New Decade, January 1959–December 1960* (Berkeley: University of California Press, 2005), pages 298–299. Also printed and verified by the American Committee on Africa, New York.

"My Talk with Ben Bella." Statement published by the *New York Amsterdam News,* New York, October 27, 1962. Transcription and verification under the title "The Ben Bella Conversation," courtesy of the library

and archives of the Martin Luther King, Jr., Center for Nonviolent Social Change, Atlanta, and Special Collections, Mugar Memorial Library, Boston University, Boston.

"The Negro Looks at Africa." Statement on colonialism and racism in Africa. Published by the *New York Amsterdam News*, New York, December 8, 1962. Transcription and verification courtesy of the library and archives of the Martin Luther King, Jr., Center for Nonviolent Social Change, Atlanta, and Special Collections, Mugar Memorial Library, Boston University, Boston.

"Palm Sunday Sermon on Mohandas K. Gandhi." Dexter Avenue Baptist Church, Montgomery, Alabama, March 22, 1959. Taken from Clayborne Carson et al., eds., *The Papers of Martin Luther King, Jr., Volume V: Threshold of a New Decade, January 1959–December 1960* (Berkeley: University of California Press, 2005), pages 145–157. Transcription and verification also courtesy of the library and archives of the Martin Luther King, Jr., Center for Nonviolent Social Change, Atlanta, and Special Collections, Mugar Memorial Library, Boston University, Boston.

"My Trip to the Land of Gandhi." Statement on King's tour of India, Chicago. Taken from *The Papers of Martin Luther King, Jr., Volume V: Threshold of a New Decade, January 1959–December 1960*, Clayborne Carson et al., eds. (Berkeley: University of California Press, 2005), pages 231–238.

"Jawaharlal Nehru, a Leader in the Long Anti-Colonial Struggle." Article prepared for *Legacy of Nehru*, a centenary volume, Atlanta, February 8, 1965. Transcription and verification courtesy of the library and archives of the Martin Luther King, Jr., Center for Nonviolent Social Change, Atlanta.

"The Octopus of Poverty." Statement on the evils of world poverty, Atlanta. Published in the *Mennonite*, January 5, 1965, page 4.

"Poverty and the World House." From Martin Luther King, Jr., *Where Do We Go from Here: Chaos or Community?* (Boston: Beacon Press, 1968), pages 176–181.

"Nonviolence and Social Change." Statement on the disinherited people of the world. From Martin Luther King, Jr., *The Trumpet of Conscience* (San Francisco: Harper & Row, 1968), pages 53–64.

"Address at the Thirty-sixth Annual Dinner of the War Resisters League." Antiwar address, New York, February 2, 1959. In Clayborne Carson et al., eds., *The Papers of Martin Luther King, Jr., Volume V: Threshold of a New Decade, January 1959–December 1960* (Berkeley: University of California Press, 2005), pages 120–125.

"The Greatest Hope for World Peace." Statements on the futility of war, Atlanta, November 5, 1964. Prepared for *Redbook Magazine.* Transcription and verification courtesy of the library and archives of the Martin Luther King, Jr., Center for Nonviolent Social Change, Atlanta.

"The Casualties of the War in Vietnam." Speech on U.S. involvement in Vietnam, the Nation Institute, Beverly-Hilton Hotel, Los Angeles, February 25, 1967. Transcription and verification courtesy of the library and archives of the Martin Luther King, Jr., Center for Nonviolent Social Change, Atlanta.

"Beyond Vietnam: A Time to Break Silence." Major speech against U.S. involvement in the war in Vietnam, New York City, April 4, 1967. Speech included in Dr. Martin Luther King Jr. et al., *Speak on the War in Vietnam* (New York: Clergy and Laity Concerned about Vietnam, 1967).

"The Middle East Question." Statement with the SCLC on the Israeli-Palestinian conflict, National Conference on New Politics, Chicago, September 1967. Transcription and verification courtesy of library and archives of the Martin Luther King, Jr., Center for Nonviolent Social Change, Atlanta.

"War and the World House." Statement on war as a threat to world community and peace. Taken from Martin Luther King, Jr., *Where Do We Go from Here: Chaos or Community?* (Boston: Beacon Press, 1968), pages 181–186.

"Christianity and African Religions." Statement contrasting Christianity with African traditional religions. In Clayborne Carson et al., eds., *The Papers of Martin Luther King, Jr., Volume IV: Symbol of the Movement, January 1957–December 1958* (Berkeley: University of California Press, 2000), pages 471–472.

"I Have Never Been a Religious Bigot." Letter denying the idea that Christianity has a monopoly on truth. Written to Mr. M. Bernard Res-

nikoff, Fairlawn, New Jersey, September 17, 1961. Transcription and verification courtesy of the library and archives of the Martin Luther King, Jr., Center for Nonviolent Social Change, Atlanta, and Special Collections, Mugar Memorial Library, Boston University, Boston.

"A Narrow Sectarianism That Causes Me Real Concern." Letter denouncing religious intolerance. Written to Dr. Harold E. Fey, editor, the *Christian Century*, Chicago, June 23, 1962. Transcription and verification courtesy of the library and archives of the Martin Luther King, Jr., Center for Nonviolent Social Change, Atlanta, and Special Collections, Mugar Memorial Library, Boston University, Boston.

"All the Great Religions of the World." Statement concerning the love ethic shared by all of the world's great religions. Prepared for publication in *Redbook Magazine*, November 5, 1964. Transcription and verification courtesy of the library and archives by Martin Luther King, Jr., Center for Nonviolent Social Change, Atlanta.

"My Jewish Brother!" Statement against anti-Semitism and on the enduring relevance of the ancient Hebrew prophets. Published in the *New York Amsterdam News*, New York, February 26, 1966, pages 1 and 12.

"Buddhists and Martyrs of the Civil Rights Movement." Joint statement with the Buddhist monk Thich Nhat Hanh concerning the common struggle shared by Buddhists in Vietnam and African Americans in the civil rights movement. Prepared under the auspices of the International Committee of Conscience on Vietnam, Nyack, New York, 1966. Transcription and verification courtesy of Martin Luther King, Jr., Center for Nonviolent Social Change, Atlanta.

EPIGRAPHS

Part I opener: From "The Three Dimensions of a Complete Life," in Clayborne Carson et al., eds., *The Papers of Martin Luther King, Jr., Volume V: Threshold of a New Decade, January 1959–December 1960* (Berkeley: University of California Press, 2005), page 576.

Part II opener: From "Doubts and Certainties," in BBC interview transcript, library and archives, Martin Luther King, Jr., Center for Nonviolent Social Change, Atlanta.

Part III opener: From "Discerning the Signs of History," library and archives, Martin Luther King, Jr., Center for Nonviolent Social Change, Atlanta.

Part IV opener: From "Pacem In Terris II Convocation" statement, library and archives, Martin Luther King, Jr., Center for Nonviolent Social Change, Atlanta.

Part V opener: Martin Luther King, Jr. (signed by his secretary Miss D. McDonald in his absence) to Mr. G. Ramachandran, editor of *Gandhi Marg*, Rajghat, New Delhi -1, India, December 20, 1961, page 1, library and archives, Martin Luther King, Jr. Center for Nonviolent Social Change, Atlanta.

Part VI opener: From "Redirecting Our Missionary Zeal," in Clayborne Carson et al., eds., *The Papers of Martin Luther King, Jr., Volume VI: Advocate of the Social Gospel, September 1948–March 1963* (Berkeley: University of California Press, 2007), page 249.

INDEX

abolitionism, 68
Acton's dictum, 156
"Address at the Thirty-sixth
 Annual Dinner of the War Resist-
 ers League" (King; 1959), 135,
 139–145
African Continent, xiv–xv, 39, 42–
 44, 54, 58–61, 80–82. *See also*
 colonialism; *specific countries*
African National Congress (ANC),
 25, 33
Albany, Georgia, xxi, 78
Alexander the Great, 157, 185
Algerian Republic, 53–54, 78–79
Ali, Muhammad, 195
"All the Great Religions of the
 World" (King; 1964), 193,
 204–5
Almond, J. Lindsay, 139
American Committee on Africa
 (ACOA), xx–xxi, 25, 30–32,
 76–77
American Friends Service Committee, 101
American Jewish Congress,
 182–183
American Negroes: Africa and,
 42–44, 54, 80–82; as ambassadors, 81; Christian, 18–19;
 freedom revolution of, 10–12,
 19–20, 78–79, 139–40; racial
 justice and, 11–12; Vietnam War
 and, 155–56; world house and,
 xiv, 9–12. *See also* civil rights
 movement
American Negro Leadership Conference on Africa (ANLCA), xx,
 26, 80–82
Americans for South African Resistance (AFSAR), 25

Anglican Students Federation
 (ASF), 27
Angola, 42, 47
annihilation, 134, 144–5, 157.
 See also arms race; nuclear proliferation
anti-revolutionary colonialism, 153
anti-Semitism, 182–83, 193–94,
 206
antiwar protest. *See* protest and
 dissent
apartheid, xiv–xv, xxi–xxii, 24–29,
 30–32, 33–35
Appeal for Action Against Apartheid (1962), xxi, 24–25, 33–35
Arden House Conference, 80–82
arms race, 119, 137, 140, 157–60,
 184–85. *See also* nuclear proliferation
Asian-African Bloc, 73, 110–11
atonement, 42, 175

Bantu Education Act, 30
Bella, Ben, 53–54, 78–79
Bellamy, Edward, 6
"Beyond Vietnam" (King; 1967),
 xxvi, 136, 164–81
Bhave, Vinoba, 107–8
Bhoodanists, 107–9
bigotry, xxvii–xxviii, 42, 190,
 192–94, 197–98, 199–203
Birmingham, Alabama, 19, 125–26
"The Birth of a New Nation"
 (King; 1957), 53, 58–75
Blackstone Rangers, 128
Blake, Eugene Carson, xxiv
blame, poverty and, 115
Bonaparte, Napoleon, 157, 185
Bond, Horace Mann, 63
Bond, Julian, xv

THE KING LEGACY SERIES

In partnership with the Estate of Dr. Martin Luther King, Jr., Beacon Press is proud to share the great privilege and responsibility of furthering Dr. King's powerful message of peace, nonviolence, and social justice with a historic publishing program—the King Legacy.

The series will encompass Dr. King's most important writings, including sermons, orations, lectures, prayers, and all of his previously published books that are currently out of print. Published accessibly and in multiple formats, each volume will include new material from acclaimed scholars and activists, underscoring Dr. King's continued relevance for the twenty-first century and bringing his message to a new generation of readers.

Clayborne Carson is general editorial advisor to the King Legacy and is director of the King Institute at Stanford University.

thekinglegacy.org

Library of Congress Cataloging-in-Publication Data
King, Martin Luther, Jr., 1929–1968.
"In a single garment of destiny" : a global vision of justice /
Martin Luther King, Jr. / edited and introduced by Lewis V. Baldwin.
p. cm.
Includes bibliographical references and index.
ISBN 978-0-8070-8605-6 (hardcover : alk. paper)
1. Human rights. 2. Civil rights. 3. Social justice.
I. Baldwin, Lewis V., 1949– II. Title.
E185.97.K5A5 2012
323—dc23   2012026882